Of Joints and Other Articulations

Of Joints and Other Articulations

The Futures of Arthrosophy

MICHAEL MARDER

Northwestern University Press

Evanston, Illinois

Northwestern University Press
www.nupress.northwestern.edu

Printed in the United States of America

10 9 8 7 6 5 4 3 2 1

Library of Congress Cataloging-in-Publication Data

Names: Marder, Michael, 1980– author.
Title: Of joints and other articulations :
the futures of arthrosophy / Michael Marder.
Description: Evanston, Illinois :
Northwestern University Press, 2026. | Includes index.
Identifiers: LCCN 2025024926 | ISBN 9780810149618 (paperback) |
ISBN 9780810149625 (cloth) | ISBN 9780810149632 (ebook)
Subjects: LCSH: Joints—Philosophy.
Classification: LCC B105.B64 M3535 2026 | DDC 128.6—dc23
LC record available at https://lccn.loc.gov/2025024926

for Ed Casey,
a wonderful teacher,
coauthor, and friend

Contents

Arthrosophy.

The Wisdom of Joints

I have always shied away from thinking, publicly speaking, and writing about "the body," a theme that has been fashionable in philosophy and social theory since the 1970s. It is not that I find the topic excessively intimate and somehow inappropriate. On the contrary, *the* body, for instance as discussed in Foucault, is too idealist an entity, too abstract to say anything meaningful about. Thus, I second the words of Jean-Luc Nancy on the subject: "The body, bodily, *never happens, least of all when it's named and convoked*. For us, the body is always sacrificed: eucharist."[1]

Whose body? This question, seeking to establish the right of ownership, is the first determinate question *of* the body in all Western philosophy, the question to which the body is sacrificed without further ado, even if it gains its meaning through this sacrifice. Who lays claim to it? But also whom or what does it claim for itself? A plant? A human? An animal? A world? A work? Is the body an "it" and, therefore, an object primed for appropriation with different degrees of mastery, contingent on the thoroughness of self-appropriation? As a concept, "the bodily" is still deformed by centuries-long corralling in the infamous mind-body split, which poisons everything on either side of the divide.[2] As the substratum of disciplining and shaping practices, it is too indeterminate to be anything but biomass. The two appearances (or non-appearances) of the body are actually tightly linked; it can be this substratum only because, despite being the target of persistent critique, the Cartesian tradition is still the prevalent paradigm for seeing and manipulating the world, for imposing a preconceived form onto what is presumed to be shapeless matter.

Things are different with respect to specific organs that, more than isolated body parts, are the body's setting to and being at work.[3] The hand, the ear, the heart, the tongue and lips, the uterus and the vagina, the circumcised penis of "circumfessions" in Merleau-Ponty, Derrida, Irigaray, Nancy, or Kristeva—authors who are, in one way or another, influenced by phenomenology—invite close philosophical attention to corporeal existence in its materiality, activity, and pathos-laden effects, the organs being substance and subject, in the work and at work. More than theoretical fetishes, in keeping with Freud's theory of the fetish as a metonymic replacement of the whole or with Klein's part-objects, these are momentary concentration points, galvanizing embodied thinking and enminded bodying outside *and* within the organism. They are, to reiterate the inversion of Deleuze and Guattari in the title of Žižek's 2004 book, "organs without bodies."

The fissure between the formal abstractness of the body and the concrete partiality of its organs (however vital to the proper functioning of the whole these might be) outlines the first horizon for thinking organismic corporeality.[4] The second such horizon coincides with another fissure, the one cutting between a closed, relatively self-enclosed living totality and an open-ended body plan of a living being prone to anarchic proliferation. Whether speaking of bodies of discourse, politics, or biological existence, the two horizons make possible and, in making possible, doubly limit *the imagination of bodily articulation*, that is, not only of how a viable body is pulled together, but also of how it keeps pulling itself together when it is alive, how it keeps articulating, disarticulating, and rearticulating itself across a range of its physiological, anatomical, environmental, grammatical, syntactic, or power structures, functions, and processes. A fragment or a systemic treatise? Empire or balkanization? Animal or plant? Stark either/or choices, which belong together on the same ontological plane, are prefabricated in the very framing of the question of the body (of the body without organs or of organs without bodies), deepening contemporary political, philosophical, aesthetic, and ecological deadlocks.

The imagination and the practice of bodily articulation cannot afford to accept only one of the two incompatible alternatives; acquiescence to either/or formulations loses sight of the articulatory aspect of corporeal composition. This is where the joints become prominent. By analogy to the primordial senses of softness and hardness as the respective *yes* and *no* of matter itself,[5] they are the *yes-no* of organismic existence. Articulations maintain what they articulate in an exemplary relation—together and apart, detached yet joined. At first glance, they seem more appropriate to vegetal organisms that thrive in a loosely bound alliance of multiple growths, shedding and adding on new organs, potentially or actually expressed at every meristem, which dynamically separates the plant from and connects it to portions of the outside world. But a closer look indicates that the decentered, multiple, indeterminately articulated bodily constitution is also prevalent in animals, who are not the walking-crawling-swimming-hopping-flying totalities they have been interpreted as, from Aristotle to Hegel.

In vertebrates, the articulations of the bones are called just that: in Romance languages, *articolazione*, *articulations*, *articulaciones*, *articulações*; in English, *joints*. These anatomical wonders are slotted between osseous structures, joining them together *and* disjoining them, introducing a degree of indeterminacy into an ostensibly closed system and rendering it mobile. They immanently de-systemize the system and let it operate as the system that it is. So, what if we regarded the body from the perspective of its joints, the essentially intermediate anatomical elements? The view from the joints outwards is actually consistent with the current scientific perspective, according to which "joints . . . are crucial components of the human frame. Indeed, they play such a pivotal role in musculoskeletal anatomy that, rather than thinking of the human skeleton as an assembly of bones, you should look upon it as a system of joints connected by lengths of levers."[6] To be sure, joints do not make up a system of their own, but, in light of the recommendation to shift perspectives, what if we encountered the body (mine, yours, ours, theirs) not by mentally drawing its silhouette or its internal framework from bone to bone, but, rather, by starting from and ending at that which is between these dense, rigid, calcium-laced units?[7] And what if we did so, also, with respect to the bodies of thought, of language, of a political assemblage, of a work, not forgetting, of course, works of art? Perhaps then fragmentation and totalization would not be the only options available within the arsenal of the bodily imaginary. Instead, the totality would internally undo itself, and isolated fragments would band together to form fleeting and flexible wholes.

...

"The being of spirit is a bone [*das Sein des Geistes ein Knochen ist*]" (*PhG* §343), wrote Hegel in *Phenomenology of Spirit* and had a hearty laugh. He marveled at how the undeniably stupid conclusions of phrenology reflect, speculatively and obliquely, the truth of spirit. This quasi-science connects the inner to the outer, a spiritual potentiality to an actual material structure, but it does so in a purely arbitrary, outer way. With a wink to Hegel's dialectical logic, we could say that the being of spirit is a joint, the discontinuous continuity of a disruption and an ordering, of putting in motion, animating fractured articulation, converting its objective frailty into strength, a strength that remains incredibly frail, non-regenerative, or at least not easily so. Assembling beings, articulating them among themselves, *logos* is a multitude of sublime joints. Philosophy is the rheumatology of spirit.

...

In his 1802 book *Natural Theology*, the deacon and fellow at Christ's College in Cambridge, William Paley, advances an argument about creation from design. Furthering Robert Boyle's analogy of God-the-watchmaker and the world-watch, Paley infers divine wisdom from the intricacy of organismic "contrivances." The body parts that arouse his absolute admiration are the joints: "To almost all the bones belong *joints* and in these, still more clearly than in the form or shape of the bones themselves, are seen both contrivance and contriving wisdom. Every joint is a curiosity, and is also strictly mechanical."[8]

For Paley, the wisdom of joints is that of God, who is their first and efficient cause. It is, in the words of "the Teutonic philosopher" Jakob Boehme, the signature of the creator etched on a created thing. But when God is out of the equation, the wisdom of joints remains—no longer as a token of superior design. What I call *arthrosophy* is this wisdom, the sagacity of the articulated body, articulating itself and/with its world. What are the main features of this articulation?

By and large, arthrosophy coincides with philosophy; more precisely, it spells out one of the senses of philosophy (which Socrates shares with earlier thinkers, including Empedocles, and which is accepted by the subsequent ones, all the way to Freudian psychoanalysis) as the love of assembling and dividing, uniting and separating. More than that, arthrosophy is a philosophy engrained, if only unconsciously, in our own bodies and minds; it is implicit in the atoms and empty spaces, DNA sequences and cells, synaptic clefts, organs and systems, languages and thoughts, environmental interactions and tools, that make us who we are. To begin with the wisdom of joints and jointures is, therefore, to begin with what is closest to us and what, for that very reason, remains in the penumbra of comprehension.

In this proximity, we would do well to remember that, just as the vertebrate organism is but one of many variations on a living animal corporeity, so, too, the joints of the skeleto-muscular system are but one conceivable articulation of bodily articulation, of *arthron* (the Greek word for "joint" or "articulation"). The same holds for wisdom (*sophia*). With respect to Aristotle (and not only him), it is fair to say that "theoretical wisdom entails the realization that human good is not the good without qualification—that what is good for humans is not necessarily *the* good. *Sophia* would, then, have to do with the good *as such*."[9] The ideality of this *as such* is highly suspect, though. Relativizing both *arthron* and *sophia*, arthrosophy begins with the wisdom of human joints, but it does not end there. Instead, almost immediately, it shifts the theoretical gaze to the joints of vertebrates, to the articulations of plants devoid of a skeleton, to those of *logos* and an artwork, of a polity and of the cosmos. *Sophia* is neither separate from nor prior to these singular instantiations of *arthron*; it is contingent on the how, the when, the where, the with-whom or with-what of each articulation.

Within any given body and across various bodies and kinds of bodies—biological, textual, social, political—joints are an irreducible multiplicity. We have more of them than we think we do. They are essentially many, in number as well as in kind, in degrees of mobility, shapes, emplacements, modes of fitting-together. In lieu of an idealized image of the "as such," the wisdom of joints is committed to this plurality of articulations (akin to philosophical categories in abstract thought) that are not uniform, each of them responding to minute place-, context-, activity-, or interactivity-bound exigencies.[10] There is no such thing as *the* joint; the *the* is itself a singular articulation, an article (the definite article), which is a variation on the theme of jointure, tying a word to *this* thing it names and no other, while untying it from the idiosyncrasy of the *this* by the very act of naming.

Joints conjoin and disjoin. They are what they do. But they also undo what they do in the instance of doing it, contradicting or counteracting themselves. Their wisdom is not quite a positive revelation of a deeper hidden truth. It is, instead, the proscription of univocal, uniform, unidirectional solution, idea, and trajectory of truth.

...

In its structuration, the present study takes its cues from the joints. Chapters considering the joints of *logos*, of time, of art, or of psychophysiological being are interspersed with those that philosophically reflect on concrete joints in a vertebrate body: hinge and ball-and-socket synovial joints, cranial sutures, and so forth. Within each chapter, there are paragraph-long inserts that act as textual joints in the book. You may read the text starting from these inserts and then proceed to the previous and subsequent sections, between which they are slotted. You may also chart a reading path beginning from chapters dedicated to the anatomical joints, while keeping in mind their connections to, and disconnects from, the materials that precede and follow them. How to read arthrologically is a practical question to be answered each time anew in the very exercise of reading.

On Knees and Elbows.

The Hinge Joints, or a Speculative Arthrology

While awaiting my turn at the rheumatology unit of a major hospital, it occurred to me that, holding the bones together and supporting (within obvious boundaries) the freedom of movement, joints are the body parts that epitomize our epoch. Even the intricate apparatus of the nervous system does not do justice to our age of connectivity and disarticulation, of linkages and dislocations, to the same degree as joints that also play a leading role in today's politics and everyday life.

Two events have hurled elbows and knees, among other joints of the extremities, into the spotlight in recent years: the COVID-19 pandemic and the homicide of George Floyd in police custody. To Shakespeare's "time is out of joint," it is now necessary to add the time *of* the joint and time *as* joints, also in their utterly disjointed form. *Our time* . . .

During the pandemic, the work of the hand—whether it was constructive or destructive, intentional or not—was delegated to the elbow. To minimize the chances of passing the new coronavirus to others, we took part in new social rituals and respiratory etiquette. An alternative way of greeting that replaced handshakes was an elbow bump, even as coughs and sneezes had to be contained in an arm folded at the elbow (and they still are). A peaceful salutation and danger converged on the same joint, with the minor nuance that the salute activated the outer side of the elbow, while biohazards were allocated to its inner pit.

Colloquially, elbows connote the space of freedom. "Elbow room" is both the physical space in which to move around and the liberty to do what one wishes. Protruding beyond the boundaries of the rib cage on both sides, elbows extend the body into its proximate environment, blazing the trail for the rest of it. Now, this freedom spearheaded by the elbows immediately becomes a tight constraint; the egoism of elbow room is identical to the altruism of protecting the other from infection. The joint is the organ where such inversions are rife, seeing that it occupies the essentially unstable position in the middle, which may suddenly lapse into one of the extremes it is slotted between.

An ever-renewed inversion, without closure, at the joint is the commerce between movement and rest, as well as between the one and the many. Aristotle illustrates these inversions with reference to the elbow in *De motu animalium*: "The origin, to which movement can be traced, qua origin, is always at rest, while the part below is in motion—the elbow joint, for instance, when the forearm is in motion" (*PA* 698b1–5).[11] But the origin at rest is itself not absolute; relative to another moving part, it too can be set in motion. A point of transition between opposites, the joint troubles hard-and-fast distinctions between them. Similarly with respect to the crucial distinction between the one and the many: while an arm as an arm is one, it is divided into two at the elbow. Hence, Aristotle concludes, "the centers in the joints are, potentially and actually [*dunamei kai energeia*], sometimes one and sometimes divided" (*PA* 698a26–b1). Fluidity in and of the center converts it into the much more unpredictable, internally decentered, middle.

Besides the elbow, another hinge joint is the knee. Already the medico-anatomic term "hinge joint" is indicative of how the body, observed from the perspectives of the joints, is both natural and artificial. It is no longer certain where the born ends and the made begins. In and of themselves, joints are not only organs fitting parts of the skeleton together (and joints may be considered organs, as recent studies of osteoarthritis contend),[12] but also points where the edges of human-made structures meet (as in welding or masonry, not to mention carpentry, where "joinery" names the aspect of woodworking to do with fitting and joining pieces of wood together) *and* points of oscillation between the born and the made.

The hinge, which lends its name to some of the joints in a vertebrate organism, is also one of the senses of *la brisure*, a keyword of deconstruction that Roger Laporte recommends to Derrida in a letter reproduced in *Of Grammatology*. Although it literally refers to a break (*briser*, "to break"), *brisure* is a rupture and a jointure, an inherently disrupted, disarticulated articulation, as in the "hinged articulation of two parts of wood- or metal-work" or in "the folding-joint of a shutter."[13] Artifice is a soft spot of the deconstructive reading, which will point out "this *brisure* of language as writing," as the very making and unmaking of the body of a written text, or, again, as that which "articulates and at the same time disarticulates the immediate unity of meaning."[14] With Shakespeare, Derrida will pivot back to joints via time, the time that is out of joint (and we will accompany him in this move, in due time). For now, suffice it to say that the body of speech as much as of writing (and, for Derrida, of speech as a disavowed sort of writing) is always articulated and disarticulated, in a way not to be dismissed for being unabashedly metaphorical, by hinge joints—knees and elbows—both in its syntaxis and in parataxis.

. . .

Joints are all about the fittingness of parts, their gathering in a togetherness without fusion, their minimal coherence and mobility: a just arrangement, adjusted to each other and to the common task. This ordering is not hierarchical. Prevailing over the relation between what is above and below is the relation of proximity and distance, of imperfect contiguity—next to . . . And the distance or the proximity of the structures that the joints interrelate is not mutually indifferent, even in technically crafted things. On either side of the joint, the fit is effective only inasmuch as one part is attuned to the other and to the gaps, clefts, crevices, cracks, crannies, fissures between them.

. . .

In the murder of George Floyd, knees were weaponized. On May 25, 2020, still at the very beginning of the pandemic period, when respiratory infections and breathing were matters of universal concern, Floyd, who was killed in cold blood by a police officer, mouthed the words "I can't breathe" more than twenty times. His death occurred after a nine-minute stretch of time when Derek Chauvin was kneeling, pressing a side of Floyd's neck down with his knee.

Just as the worst and the best, the promising and the dangerous, were aggregated in the elbow, so these opposites were gathered together and revolved around actions centered on the knee joint. In the subsequent widespread protests against police brutality all over the United States, numerous officers, including NYPD chief Terence Monahan, "took the knee" alongside the protesters. The practice of taking the knee was, of course, pioneered by American athletes during the playing of the national anthem at sporting events in order to highlight racial injustice in the country. Before and after Floyd's murder, the same position of the leg's hinge joint was meant to speak out, silently, against the kind of behavior that culminated in his death. As such, the knee is charged with the potential for speculative reversals.

A bent knee signals allegiance and enslavement, prayerful devotion and brutal pressure, intended if not to kill then to torture (as in forcing someone to kneel on rice, corn grains, or buckwheat seeds, where the baneful joint is not the knee of the other, but one's own, or in embarking on a painful, penitent pilgrimage by "walking" hundreds of kilometers on one's knees and then climbing up, still on the knees, the stairs that lead up to the Sanctuary of Our Lady of the Rosary of Fátima in Portugal). Bending and straightening (that is to say, flexion and extension) are actually the main functions of hinge joints, such as knees and elbows. Ontically broken, and in their brokenness facilitating the movements of the limbs, they are also ontologically broken, disrupting the straightforward relations of valuation and causality.

In *De incessu animalium*, Aristotle links bending (*kampsin*) at the joint with animal movement: "If there were no bending, there would be no walking or swimming or flying. For since animals with feet stand and rest their weight alternately on each of their two opposite legs, as one leg advances, the other must necessarily be bent. . . . But since the legs are equal, the leg which is at rest must bend either at the knee or, in any kneeless animal that walks, at the joint" (*PA* 708b25–35).[15] An upright position in movement requires one to abandon the rigid stance, the erect posture, before reestablishing it and losing it again continuously, with every step one takes. The knee guarantees this loss *and* preservation of positions, be they spatial or moral. It is the place of physical and metaphysical metabolisms (the change from straight to bent and back again is a case of *metabolê*; *PA* 708b25) in the making of the human.

Crawling is apparently more "straightforward," but in human beings it, too, depends on bending at other joints: "It is possible," Aristotle continues, "to move even if the leg has no bend in it, as happens when children crawl. Movement of this kind takes place through a bending in the shoulders and hips. But no creature could walk erect in this way continuously and safely, but only move like those who drag themselves forward through the dust in the wrestling school on their knees" (*PA* 709a8–15). The secure support of the ground for a crawling animal (and for a human baby) comes with a steep price tag: the one who crawls descends to the level of invertebrates, constantly in touch with the earth and its dust, dragging oneself through it. Straightness is dehumanization in a rigidly upright stance, which is ideally unmovable, *and* in the horizontality of crawling. This dehumanization is the most intimate possibility of human beings and of being human, the possibility out of which the human emerges and back into which it dips time and again.

Today, rather than merely ensure the flexion and extension of limbs, granting them the freedom of movement within the anatomical limits of bones, muscles, and ligaments, elbows and knees take charge of acting. Articular action is concurrent with a counteraction; every articulation is, simultaneously, a disarticulation, which is just as (if not more) active. This simultaneity, reminiscent of but irreducible to Newton's third law, has not yet been grasped at the level of consciousness—or barely so. In a scaled-down version of planetary developments, it has to do with the hypostasis of negativity, with negativity's twisting free from the space-time of a relation and striving to absoluteness, to the absolute disjointedness of the dump-world. With this in mind and recovering the double negative encoded in the word itself, disruption should come to signify un-breaking, a rearticulation, above all, of articulation itself. And hinge joints are a good place to start.

...

Nancy on Derrida: "'The joint is a *brisure* ['hinge'].' The system, then, really is a system, but a system of *brisure*. This is not the negation of system, but system itself, suspended at the point of its *systasis*. *Brisure* does not break the joint: in repetition 'nothing has budged.' Or else, the joint has always already been broken in itself, as such and in sum by itself. What joins divides; what adjoins is divided. *Brisure* is not the other of juncture, it is its heart, its essence, and its passion. It is the exact and infinitely discrete limit upon which the joint articulates itself."[16]

...

The actions and counteractions of knees and elbows write a fresh chapter in the story of a being who is still, by force of habit, known as *human*. To recap, from an evolutionary, anthropological, or arthrological perspective, the upright posture liberated the hands of our ancestors in a self-perpetuating cycle of humanization. Early humans were humanized by the work of their hands, which was made possible by the development of bipedalism, such that the hands were no longer used for supporting or relocating the body in space. In the bipedal position, the knees bear most of the body's weight. The knee joints assume the rest of the body; they take it upon themselves, subtending the freedom of the hand. They bear corporeal mass and responsibility for the responsibility, with which hands have been entrusted.

Kneeling is a symbolic act of consciously giving up the physical (and the associated moral) uprightness of the human stance, of relieving or, on the contrary, aggravating the weight of the body and of responsibility. It can mean the humility of coming back down to earth or descent into the whirlpools of violence and raw force with its wordless proclamation of the right of the strongest. Further, humility balances on a razor-thin edge with humiliation; economically and politically humiliated nations—for instance, as a result of defeat in a war or externally imposed austerity measures—perceive themselves as being collectively on their knees, whereas the act of rising from their knees is often wrapped in belligerent nationalist discourse, replete with exclusionary (and, on occasion, genocidal) policies.

In their turn, the actions of elbows free the very hands that had been freed for activity by virtue of bipedalism. Hand-free headsets may free the hand *from* something *for* something else (here, from holding a cellphone and for driving or cooking). But when hands are freed for nothing in particular, for inaction, permitting elbows to do their work, they may engage in the art of non-doing (the Taoist *wùwei* or the positively fruitless practice leading to liberation, *mokṣa*, in Indian traditions) *or* they may succumb to the controversial post-human condition, where incredible technological advances coincide with the pronounced loss of fine motor skills and finger dexterity in children.

My point is that the role knees and elbows play in political events with global resonance and in subtler mutations of habitual behavior is not at all accidental. But if the focus of action shifts to knees and elbows, so should the locus of thinking. Instead of thinking with our hands in an effort to combine theory and practice and instead of thinking on our feet, we should start thinking on our knees and elbows, with our elbows and knees. What might the thinking of the joints feel and look like? How to think not only about joints, but also with joints, through and across them? How to do so while not losing sight of the fact that being-with is a matter of the joint, of jointure as a broken articulation, a disarticulation within articulation that activates gathering without fusion?

One relation which is dismantled or undergoes drastic reconfiguration in the unexpected activity of the hinge joints is a strict correspondence of structures and functions. When knees are used to kill or to kneel, when elbows absorb viral emissions or greet friends, they do something that is not functionally preprogrammed in articular anatomical formations. In other words, joints no longer perform the tasks they are to fulfil within the system of which they are a part and which they dynamically form from their intermediate positions between the bones. Instead, they disrupt, disjoin, and reconfigure the system from within, immanently.

In one way or another, cultural activity entails a persistent negotiation and a practical reinterpretation of bodily structure-function relations. *What to do with our bodies and with the bodies of others?* is an open question, shadowed but not determined by biological constraints. For instance, knee clasping was a practice which made perfect sense in ancient Greece but which may appear rather opaque to us. Mentioned both in the *Iliad* and in the *Odyssey*, it is a gesture of supplication. When Odysseus returns home, he finds his wife surrounded by numerous suitors. First, one of the suitors, Leodes, begs Odysseus to spare his life, while clasping the hero's knees (*Od.* 22.310–19). Then Phemius, the minstrel who entertained the suitors, repeats the same gesture (*Od.* 22.333–37). Performatively, each of them proclaims: "I clasp your knees [*gounoûmai*]" (*Od.* 22.312, 22.344). Odysseus kills Leodes (by decapitation) and spares Phemius. In the *Iliad*, Priam, the king, asks Achilles to take pity on him: "Great Priam entered in, and coming close to Achilles, clasped in his hands his knees [*Achillêos lábe gounata*], and kissed his hands, the terrible, man-slaying hands that had slain his many sons" (*Il.* 24.475–80).

German scholars classified ritually coded knee clasping as *Kontaktmagie*; clasping the knee alludes to clasping an altar in a supplicatory gesture addressed to a god.[17] On a corporeal plane, however, holding onto the hinge joints of the limbs prevents their movement, which is what the supplicant typically seeks, namely to avert an action spelling out disaster. The use of handcuffs in police arrests also blocks limb movements by way of limiting the freedom of the joints (here: of the wrists; in other cases: of the ankles, by resorting to shackles). Conversely, the direct actions and counteractions of knees and elbows are deaf to supplication, as it became agonizingly clear in the murder of George Floyd.

...

It is an extraordinary situation. Hinge joints become not only the subject but also the substance of historical processes, actually expressing a truth of the twenty-first century. In the long term, this situation is unsustainable, in that hinge joints cannot provide fundamental support, bearing the full weight of the body and the weight of responsibility. The support they offer to a vertebrate organism in motion is fragile and tenuous; the fragility and tenuity of the joints *are* their strength. Placing the entire burden on knees and elbows, on knees *or* elbows, is redolent of punishment, even torture, in religion as much as in politics. The elbows fare better than the knees, though, to the extent that their variable positions contrast with the fixed position of the knees and with the intolerable pressure they bear, not to mention their compression between the rest of the body and the floor, the ground, or another body. The joint is out of joint; the hinge is unhinged. But this is the very being-joint of the joint, the being-hinge of the hinge.

...

If structure-function correlations crumble, then the self-understanding of arthrology needs to change. A textbook definition states: "Arthrology is the study of joints. It, perhaps more than any other subject of anatomy, illustrates the close relationship between structure and function, for arthrology is the study of how bones are joined to permit (or prevent) movement."[18] The tightest relationship between structure and function is observable in a machine or a usable artifact, even if the range of potential uses always exceeds the officially prescribed ones. This relation or correlation is loosened in living systems.

Like plants, joints have been imagined in modernity by analogy with machine parts; their precise mechanical "design" and their deterioration with age, which has been ascribed to "wear and tear," are part of this discursive construction. Things get a little more complicated when joints are viewed as organs, and the diseases associated with them are regarded as organ-level maladies. In this respect, osteoarthritis "is not simply a process of wear and tear, but rather, an abnormal remodeling of joint tissues driven by a host of inflammatory mediators within the affected joint."[19] As organs, joints continually produce and reproduce themselves in the course of organismic existence. Here, too, they are the subjects and the substance of biological processes.

The disjointedness of joints is essential to their functioning. Not even sutures, or the apparently immovable joints in the vault of the skull, are seamless continuations of the bones. They connect and disconnect, disconnect by connecting and connect by disconnecting. The joints make osseous density breathable; they enliven the inorganic heritage of the body in its skeletal frame, both inside the bone and outside. Are their effects not reminiscent of solidarity in isolation, which many experienced during the pandemic, or of solitude in the midst of social media technologies and the apparently all-embracing virtual networks? The logic of relationality, which eschews fusion as much as segregation, announces itself in this description. As does the logic of logic, the *logos* that gathers without totalizing.

The thinking of the joints and of relations is contradictory, because it belongs in the space in-between (bones, and not only). Curiously, *the* philosopher of contradiction, Hegel, does not mention joints in his *Philosophy of Nature*, where he considers in excruciating detail other aspects of "the animal organism." Within "the osseous system," joints problematize the distinction between the inner and the outer, as well as the qualities of firmness and supportiveness: "the *osseous system*, a covering for what is *inner*, and a firm support for the inner against the *outer*."[20] I have mused, with and against Hegel, that the being of spirit is the joint. I can now add that its dialectical effectivity is determinate negation (*bestimmte Negation*), destabilizing solid structures, functions, and their objective correlations and, at the same time, shaping the dynamic content and form of a body (of an organism, a polity, a text, a thought, a world) under the sign of concrete freedom. Hegel nonetheless omits joints from his *Philosophy of Nature*. Perhaps he silently discerns in them the living architecture of dialectics as such. (In the brackets, which he opens in *Language and Death* and which I want to reopen in the closing lines of this chapter, Agamben undersigns this possibility: "When Hegel conceives of the negative as *Aufhebung*, he is thinking of the *arthron* as this invisible unification, which is stronger than the visible one because it constitutes the most intimate vital pulsation—*Lebenspuls*—of every existing being.")[21]

Logos.

A Dis/Jointure

A fresh look at the body from the joints outwards discovers incompletion at the core of an apparently closed organismic system. The articulations are highly attuned to the structures they articulate, but they do not amount to a greater whole, which would overwhelm its parts. This is the most vegetal perspective imaginable on an animal organism: plants, we might say, *are all joints* (both actual and potential, i.e., the meristems); they are always ready to receive new organs, or to lose the ones they had, to disarticulate and to rearticulate themselves and their relation to the world.

Something of the vegetal perspective on the joint is visible in Confucian thought. One of the most important virtues, *jie* (节), which means fidelity, constancy, rectitude, and moderation, is designated with the character of "the joint of a bamboo stalk, metaphorically indicating stages in the direction of one's ethical life-journey, just as the joints connect the empty sections of the bamboo."[22] Although the upright position of a bamboo stalk is alluded to, the key is not this position itself but the vegetal joints that articulate parts of the plant in an appropriate manner. Moral integrity has to do with how one articulates parts of one's life and actions that are visible only in their incomplete, segmented, sectioned composition. These, as a matter of fact, are the other senses of *jie*—section, segment, part, joint—that give the word a dialectically speculative air, letting it say and unsay, contra-dict, itself.

Although, when transposed from a vegetal to an animal organism, an endless proliferation of limbs tends to conjure up the image of a monstrosity, this articular open-endedness is present in human life, as well. If the tools we use are the limbs of a prosthetic god, as Freud refers to modern humanity—"Man has, as it were, become a kind of prosthetic God. When he puts on all his auxiliary organs he is truly magnificent; but those organs have not grown on to him and they still give him much trouble at times" (*SE* 21: 91–92)[23]—then there must exist the natural-artificial joints, ready to receive these techno-organs. In fact, the biological organs of action, the five *karma indriyas* of the yogic tradition—*vak* (the organ of speech), *pani* (hands), *pada* (feet), *upashtam* (the organ of generation), and *payu* or *guda* (anus, the organ of excretion)—are joints between the living-breathing body and the world at large. That is why joints can stand, metonymically, for limbs and for any organ, even the internal ones, in ancient Greek, as well.[24]

In *Historia animalium*, Aristotle uses the word *arthron* to denote the genitals, as in *HA* 504b23, and other organs. To this usage, he adds the sense of vocal articulation, *arthron tês phônês*, as in *HA* 536a3, where he discusses the sounds produced by dolphins: "For this creature has a voice (and can therefore utter vocal or vowel sounds), for it is furnished with a lung and a windpipe; but its tongue is not loose, nor has it lips, so as to give utterance to an articulate sound (or a sound of vowel and consonant in combination)."[25] The articulation of sounds is the production of vocal emissions through the collaboration of the lungs, the windpipe, the tongue, and lips in the assemblage of vowels and consonants. Within the textual economy of *Historia animalium*, and of Aristotle's thought as a whole, the speech of the body, emanating from the synchronized activity of various organs, partially overlaps with the body of speech, notably with *logos* as an incorporated, carnal entity. The two bodies share the articulations, or the joints, that endow them with minimal coherence.

This is more than an analogy, let alone a metaphor (not to forget: *analogia* itself, in the way it brings together disparate elements, is subject to the dynamics of *logos*). The joint is a *jointure* between the speech of the body and the body of speech; therefore, in itself, it is more than itself. Given that joints are articulations, in the double sense of meaningful expression and of putting together things such as sounds or letters or bones, they do the work of *logos*, which denotes speaking and putting together, arranging, ordering (*legein, legô*). *Logos* is an articulation of articulations, but since joints cannot be gathered into a system, the difference between the assembly in and of *logos* and the jointure signaled by *arthron* is not a qualitative one. Its configurations are *confugurations*—fugal, fugacious, dis- and re-assembling assemblages, a persevering *with* the fugue, *with* the fleeing, *with* the no-thing whipped up in its trail.

. . .

We reencounter all sorts of bodies in a new light when they appear to us from the perspective of the joints or articulations. These include biological organisms, to be sure: plants approached starting from the meristems, the nodes, or the internodes; animals considered across their synovial joints (such as hinge joints, as well as other articular structures—the pivot, ball-and-socket, and other joints—that are equipped with a cavity and typically permit movement, often in more than one direction and along one or more axes)[26] . . . But there are also the bodies of speech, of discourse, of the text, whose joints are the breath (exhalation and inhalation in the act of vocalizing), the syntax and the parataxis, the grammar, paragraph breaks, section and chapter endings and beginnings, the articles—definite and indefinite—that individuate a noun as *this* and no other or as *any* one whatsoever of its kind. What if we were to attend to speech by taking guidance from the moments of drawing breath between sentences or spoken words? What would a text look like if we were to read it moving to the right and to the left of a full stop, or up and down with regard to a paragraph break? Freud had a comparable approach to the body of the unconscious, which, since his initial forays into the field of psychic energy, he interpreted starting from cathexes, the knots, or bound quanta of energy that function very much like joints within the structure of the libidinal body. Kant's categories may be envisioned as the joints of cognizing. And what about a body politic? Would interpreting this composite, tense, and friction-ridden body from the standpoint of civil society be equivalent to seeking its joints? Mediations are not continuous bridges, least of all in dialectics; they are the joints that connect and disrupt that which they bring together.

...

A virtuoso of analogies, Plato compares the organization of *logos* to that of a living being, *zôon*, in *Phaedrus*. Addressing Phaedrus, Socrates says: "But I do think you will agree to this, that every discourse [*panta logon*] must be organized like a living being [*zōon*], with a body of its own, as it were, so as not to be headless [*akephalon*] or footless [*apoun*], but to have a middle [*mesa te echein*] and members, composed in fitting relation to each other and to the whole." "Certainly," Phaedrus agrees (*Ph.* 264c).[27]

The living being implicit in the Socratic description is an animal: it has a head and feet, between which the middle is slotted; its members are proportionally arranged; the difference and interrelation between the whole creature and its organs is clearly delineated. And it is a particular kind of animal—a land-based vertebrate—which is of the same kind as the human. A worm-discourse or a fish-discourse would not fit the mold presented by Socrates: the former has no members, whereas the latter has no feet.

To reiterate, *logos* is an animal that lives, that nourishes itself and others, reproduces, and survives all the better the more its vertebrate animality is guaranteed and respected. It often dies, too, but can be reanimated by breath in reading out loud or by the gaze scanning a text. Its head is the introduction, the feet correspond to a conclusion, and the middle is *contained* between the two extremes, both located between them and prevented from overgrowing the body it is a part of. The universality of the description, presumably applicable to *all* logos (*panta logon*), does not, therefore, match the singularity of its biological structure. Not only is the creature an animal, rather than, say, a plant, but it is also a member of a particular subphylum, Vertebrata, within the animal kingdom.

This animal—evidently vertebrate—*logos* will survive at least up until the philosophies of Kant and Hegel. Toward the end of the first *Critique*, Kant contemplates "the architectonic of pure reason," which is at the same time aligned with the animal organism in its articulated, jointed structure and distanced from the model of vegetal growth. The system as "the unity of the manifold cognitions under one idea" is a whole that is "articulated (*articulatio*) and not heaped together (*coacervatio*); it can, to be sure, grow internally (*per intus susceptionem*) but not externally (*per appositionem*), like an animal body, whose growth does not add a limb but makes each limb stronger and fitter for its end without any alteration of proportion" (*CPR* A833/B861).[28] Kant is loath to acknowledge, of course, that the self-articulation of plants corresponds neither to internal growth nor to a heaping together of organs, and that external articulation "by apposition" is also a co-belonging of the manifold, albeit not under one idea or one central principle. The "alteration of proportion" in vegetal growth is the dynamic *ana-logos* that concentrates on the activity of articulating, rather than on the unitary principle to which the entire system may be reduced. Were Kant willing to contemplate the vegetal articulations of pure reason in its architectonic structuration, would this reason have been or become less allergic to otherness, to exteriority presenting a fresh opportunity for articulation, rather than a threat to the existing organization and proportions of the system?

For his part, Plato does not speculate on how parts of the discursive body are connected; he merely underlines their correct ordering, as well as the proportionality—itself a variation on the theme of *analogia*—of the relation among organs (of action) and between these and the whole organism. The ordering of *logos* depends on two principles that lend it "clearness and consistency": "that of perceiving and bringing together [*sunorônta*] in one idea the scattered particulars" (*Ph.* 265d) and "that of dividing things again by classes, where the joints [*kat' arthra*] are, and not trying to break any apart, after the manner of a bad carver" (265e).[29] Synthesis and analysis, bringing together and dividing, do not refer to a simple, unitary principle for the ordering and operationality of *logos*. In them, as them, articulation comes into effect. The articulation of articulation and disarticulation is both their simultaneity and their rhythmic alternation or alteration, setting the variable paces or tempos of thinking, which includes perception and ideation. The life of the living being that is *logos* depends on this rhythm, the inhalation and exhalation, the systolic and diastolic pressures of its beating heart, with a break in the beat also, and in the first place, bridging these two moments. In thought and in matter—in the one as much as in the other, as well as between the two—the conjunction and the disjunction of the joint (its "disjunctive unity") is the dynamic principle of vitality.

...

Joints animate. They enable the movements of articulated vertebrate bodies and they imbue with life the texts, organisms, psyches, or communities that form around them, around the empty spaces and ligatures, the buffers of cartilage and the punctuations (including the typographical point, the full stop in a sentence) between two or more surfaces or lines, the cathected knots of the unconscious and the mesh of civil society. These animating junctures are spatial as much as temporal: levers and rhythms, hinges and tempos, swivels and instants.

...

The analytic procedure of thinking "according to the joints" (*kat' arthra*) resonates with the story of a good cook, preserved in the writings of Zhuang Zhou, a younger contemporary of Plato who lived in China during the Warring States period. In a text titled "The Secret of Caring for Life," the cook named Ding explains:

> A good cook changes his knife once a year—because he cuts. A mediocre cook changes his knife once a month—because he hacks. I've had this knife of mine for nineteen years and I've cut up thousands of oxen with it, and yet the blade is as good as though it had just come from the grindstone. There are spaces between the joints, and the blade of the knife has really no thickness. If you insert what has no thickness into such spaces, then there's plenty of room—more than enough

> for the blade to play about in. That's why after nineteen years the blade of my knife is still as good as when it first came from the grindstone.[30]

Instead of Plato's carver, Zhuang Zhou acquaints his readers with a cook, who works with animal flesh. Supplanting an artisan, who is nonetheless obliged to respect the joints of matter itself while creating carved objects, the cook presents the model of a knowing situated closer to life, to the body of an animal, in which ancient Greeks recognized the outlines of *logos*. The cutting, which the cook Ding invokes, is *sui generis*: we may call it "cutting without cutting," and it is the reason behind the persistent sharpness of the blade after nineteen years of use. The non-violent, non-forcible separation of animal parts is due to the fact that these parts are *already* separated in the way that they are articulated—precisely at the joints.

The knife and the analytic knowing it symbolizes do not carve out the contours of bodies but seek the minuscule empty spaces of articular connections (especially synovial cavities) and reaffirm the splitting that is already there in the things themselves. Because its blade "has really no thickness," the slicing of the void in the middle of joints erases the distinction between the material and the immaterial, the spatial and the nonspatial, the real and the ideal. Ding's knife cuts without cutting to the extent that it touches without touching there where the things themselves are in touch with themselves without rubbing at their edges, there where the disjointure of joints is most palpable and a void persists in the thick of reality.

However experienced, a cook only comes across meat and bones, the chopped-up corpse of an animal, which is to say that the finest procedures of knowing according to the Way (of the joints) still only performs an autopsy. But it is by no means certain that the cook is a purely living subject confronting a dead object. Ding (鼎) is both a proper and a common name; as the latter, it is the ancient Chinese cauldron, typically replete with two facing handles on the rim and a standing support of three or four legs.[31] It is the cook in Zhuang Zhou's story, as well as the cooking pot, a master of culinary arts and an implement. The name is a joint between animate and inanimate realities. It divides and conjoins, brings together in separating and separates in bringing together the cooking agents, the cauldron and the chef. More radically, the knife's obedience to the preexisting veins of voiding in the body it cuts is a sign of how things divide and recombine themselves, all by themselves. Human beings merely need to observe, with utmost attention, these divisions and re-combinations, and to put themselves in their service. Now, this amounts to saying that the world thinks itself by itself, analyzing and synthesizing itself across its joints without a modicum of indifference, or, positively put, with the utmost care for life (the title of the ancient Chinese story), even after death. Conceptually translated into Greek, Zhuang Zhou unveils the *logos* of the world.

With all its attendant problems and glitches, conceptual translation goes both ways, of course, and what I have proposed as a reconstructed view of *logos* from the perspective of its joints is, within the Taoist outlook of Zhuang Zhou, the makeup of the body. "The hundred joints, the nine openings, the six organs, all come together and exist here [as my body]," states the "Discussion on Making All Things Equal."[32] The hollows and the holes are not simple absences in the heavy and heaving plenitude of the flesh. Their inner and outer openness defines the body, which accretes around the joints, around the openings, around the sense organs. In their dispersed multiplicity (measured by hundreds), joints are the first to be mentioned among these gaps.

Returning to the cook Ding, we notice that a vision of the body from the joints outwards and the practice corresponding to this vision follow the Way (道, *Tao* or *Dao*), which is the self-articulation of the world. "What I care about is the Way, which goes beyond skill. When I first began cutting up oxen, all I could see was the ox itself. After three years I no longer saw the whole ox. And now—now I go at it by spirit and don't look with my eyes. Perception and understanding have come to a stop and spirit moves where it wants. I go along with the natural makeup, strike in the big hollows, guide the knife through the big openings, and follow things as they are. So I never touch the smallest ligament or tendon, much less a main joint."[33] The skilled cook, who "goes beyond skill," no longer sees either the whole ox or parts of the animal, but the hollows, openings, and joints observed with an altogether different vision, guided by spirit, as opposed to perception or understanding. Yet, the spirit in question is not elevated above the things themselves; it is not distinct from things in the world that accrete around their hollows, around the void. To follow it is to "follow things as they are," the objective place of spirit localizable in the joints.

...

"A joint—can the place of spirit be as low as that?" you may wonder. "How can joints embody spirit if they often suffer from arthritis and arthrosis, are nearly mechanical in their functioning, prone to wear and tear in old age, bound to decompose with the rest of the body?" You would then be repeating, with a slight variation, the questions Master Dongguo raised before Zhuang Zhou:

> "This thing called the Way—where does it exist?"
> Zhuang Zhou said, "There's no place it doesn't exist."
> "Come," said Master Dongguo, "you must be more specific!"
> "It is in the ant."

"As low a thing as that?"
"It is in the panic grass."
"But that's lower still!"
"It is in the tiles and shards."
"How can it be so low?"
"It is in the piss and shit."[34]

...

To be a lover of wisdom—in short, to be a philosopher—one must be a lover of joints. At any rate, that is what Socrates professes in *Phaedrus* right after recommending thinking *kat' arthra*. "Now I myself, Phaedrus," says Socrates, "am a lover [*erastês*] of these processes of division and bringing together, as what enables speaking and discerning [*legein te kai phroneîn*]" (*Ph.* 266b).[35] We are here in the presence of the Socratic way, the Tao of Socrates, who continues, citing Homer's *Odyssey*: "and if I think any other man is able to see things [in this manner] . . . , him I follow after and 'walk in his footsteps as if he were a god.'" To speak and to discern, *legein* and *phroneîn*, is to obey the logic of bringing together and setting apart respectively, just as, on the figurative or figural plane, the substantification of these activities in another being, human or divine, awakens the desire to follow such a being. Understood as speech, *logos* is only one among many kinds of assembling; comprehended as discernment, *phronesis* is but one among various types of differentiation or division. It is their inimitable togetherness, though—the togetherness of togetherness and apartness—that is the object of Socratic love, namely a joint.

Arthron is the principle of two principles, and, therefore, a non-principle, an anarchic implosion of the principle and of the authority it commands from the beginning and in every instance of its setting to work. It operates by acting and, at the same time, counteracting itself, articulating and disarticulating, extending and breaking the architectures of a skeleton, saying and unsaying. This is what happens when something or someone essentially intermediate, disrupted by itself and activated by such a disruption, is pinpointed as the principle, for instance, of synthesis and analysis.

The workings of the dialectical joint (and this is, indeed, the matter of dialectics, the art of dialecticians, those quasi-divine masters of separation and assembly called *dialektikoús* [*Ph.* 266c][36]) are anything but dispassionate. Giving off the appearance of a mechanical process, these workings emerge in the midst of a discussion of love and madness, of *mania*, divided and gathered "like a body [*hôsper de sômatos*]" into "double oneness" or "unitary doubleness," *hênos diplâ*. Arranged in their derangement. The two aspects are the right and the left, a right-handed love and madness and a left-handed love and madness. The body of discourse, of *logos* which is at the heart of *Phaedrus*, displays this same separation and assembly, its body, too, materializing around the dialectical joint, which is neither one nor many and both one and many. Thinking no longer emanates exclusively from, nor is it dictatorially governed by, the head. Theory becomes arthroscopy, ineluctably tinged with the also-double affective force of love and madness.

The dialectical joint becomes purely technical and mechanical at the hands of the sophists, who excel in "the art of speech." Socrates contrasts the techno-*logos* of the sophists with his own zoo-*logos*, a discourse, speech, words that belong not to rhetorical, oratorical, and demagogic arts, but to the order of life, of breath as animation, of a living body organized in truth, by a vital truth, which is complex, articulated, jointed and disjointed, dynamic. As he notes earlier in the dialogue: "He who knows not the truth, but pursues opinions, will, it seems, attain an art of speech [*logōn ara technēn*] which is ridiculous, and not an art at all [*atechnon*]" (*Ph.* 262c).[37] Art is not art without life, emanating here from true seeing or a knowing ideation, *alētheian . . . eidos*, and not from a hunt after opinions, correct as these may be. The technology of *logos* is, in other words, a perverted subspecies of *logos*'s zoology, drained of love or bent on sublimating, diverting this love to other extraneous objects that are monetary, honor- and status-related, and so forth.

The bone of contention Socrates chews on with the sophists resurfaces, with undeniable differences, in Plato's quarrel with the poets. *Logos* sees itself beleaguered from two sides, rehashing the scheme of left- and right-handed kinds of madness: sophistic *technē*, on the one hand, and poetic *muthos*, on the other. Could this double beleaguerment signal, rather than the corruption and ultimate fall of philosophy, the joint-structure of its being, its irreducibility either to the sheer possession of wisdom or to madly erotic poetic inspiration? If so, then the philosophical battle against the sophists and the quarrel with the poets would not be an up-front standoff or a pure opposition. Philosophy is and is not sophistry; it is and is not mythopoetic discourse.

. . .

Joints mobilize and imbue with fragility. More than that, they imbue the body with fragility to the extent that they put it in motion. This confluence of enabling and disabling in the joints is part and parcel of their dialectical makeup. Ecology is the articulation of a dwelling, the *logos* of *oikos*. Its fragility is the fragility of joints, the very relations responsible for its dynamism and for the instability, insecurity, impermanence of its assemblages. Today's fittingly articulated planetary dwelling may become uninhabitable and disarticulated tomorrow; in fact, the possibility of its disarticulation is there already today, it was there yesterday, and it is what makes articulation itself possible. Only divided can a house stand. Far from an immanently undifferentiated whole, the body of Gaia is a composite multiplicity, which is growing arthritic (with the attendant inflammations, stiffness, tenderness, aches and pains) day by day.

...

One or two? Two in one or one in two? How to count a joint? And the parts of the body it articulates?

Aristotle puzzles over similar questions in the *Metaphysics*. At issue are the continuous and the discrete, *suneches* and *diôrismenon*, which in his *Categories* refer to the two modalities of quantity (*Cat.* 4b20–21). Aristotle notes, in a passage that is worth citing at length:

> Of these things themselves those which are naturally continuous are one in a truer sense than those which are artificially continuous. 'Continuous' means that whose motion is essentially one, and cannot be otherwise; and motion is one when it is indivisible, i.e., indivisible in *time*. Things are essentially continuous which are one not by contact only; for if you put pieces of wood touching one another you will not say that they are *one* piece of wood, or body, or any other continuous thing. And things which are completely continuous are said to be 'one' even if they contain a joint, and still more those things which contain no joint; e.g., the shin or the thigh is more truly one than the leg, because the motion of the leg may not be one. And the straight line is more truly one than the bent. We call the line which is bent and contains an angle both one and not one, because it may or may not move all at once; but the

> straight line always moves all at once, and no part of it which has magnitude is at rest while another moves, as in the bent line. (*Met.* 1016a1–20)[38]

Since indivisibility in space is a non-starter (space is immanently and infinitely divisible), Aristotle transfers the indivisibility of continuous entities to the order of time: they are "indivisible according to time [*adiaretos de kata chronon*]." Their temporal continuity makes them one, which is why their articulated structure, mediated by a joint, does not matter. Or, better yet, it does matter, but not so much. There are, Aristotle suggests, degrees of continuity and discreteness, intermediate cases between "one" and "not one," such as a bent line or a limb with joints. According to this line of argumentation, "the shin or the thigh is more truly one than the leg," that is to say, a part of the leg is more genuinely one than the whole, because those parts are presumably simpler than the whole, in that they evince no articulated complexity. But, given that Aristotle has relocated the question of continuity to the order of time, instead of anatomical structures, movements (i.e., sequentially assumed positions) become the litmus tests of oneness—with parts moving all at once, in a unison—and not oneness—with parts pursuing their disparate trajectories.

It is by no means certain that time is home to indivisibility and pure continuity. In the *Physics*, Aristotle himself postulates that instants are the points of time, both (literally) punctuating and extending the timelines comprising them. The lines of time are always broken, bent at every point, at every one among the infinity of its joints, potentially or actually turning the other way than the expected direction of elongation would lead one to believe. In addition, categorial indistinction reigns where it is unclear if quantities are discrete or continuous, a number or a figure, lacking or sharing a common limit. Dialectical through and through, joints baffle the kind of thinking that the ancient dialectic of the one and the many presupposes.

Among discrete quantities Aristotle includes not only numbers but also parts of speech, of spoken *logos*. In *Categories*, he observes: "Thus is number discrete, not continuous. The same may be said about speech [*kai o logos tôn diôrismenôn estin*], if by speech the spoken word is intended. Being measured in long and short syllables, speech is an evident quantity, whose parts possess no common boundary [*horos*]. No common boundary exists, where those parts—that is, syllables—join [*sullabai sunaptousin*]. Each, indeed, is distinct from the rest" (*Cat.* 4b32–40).[39] In its phonic instantiation, *logos* is bereft of form. Having no figuration, it diverges drastically from Plato's *logos* imagined as a living being. But, whatever the intended sense of *logos*, it alludes to a gathering, an assembly, a bringing together. What does a gathering of discrete parts that "possess no common boundaries" entail?

The togetherness of syllabic elements is one where they do not border on one another, do not touch. Though not touching, they are articulated. The model for this touchless articulation and communication is provided by the synapses that fire across microscopic gaps between the dendrites of one neuron and another (or between a neuron and a muscle cell at the neuromuscular junction). *Sunaptein* is, in fact, the verb Aristotle reiterates: "syllables join together [*sullabai sunaptousin*]"; "parts join [*moria sunaptei*]." A speculative dialectical word, *synapsis* says "conjunction," or "with-fastening" (*sun* + *haptein*) for the unfastened nexus of a touchless activation. It is beside the point that the tiny gaps between the terminal and reception points of neurons would not have been technically available to observation when the term was coined. Having otherwise nothing in common, joints and synapses elude direct contact (of bones, of cells' walls, etc.). Their articulations are possible thanks to disarticulation, a gathering and a togetherness without a shared boundary, which Aristotle attributes to certain aspects of *logos*. So, the body is not wiped out in discrete quantities: joints or synapses are left behind, if without the rest of fleshy extension.

...

There is more to the relation between joints and synapses than meets the eye. *Hapsos* is a synonym of *arthron*; both mean "joint." In the *Odyssey*, when Penelope is overtaken by sleep, it is said that "all her joints [*hapsei panta*] relaxed" (*Od.* 4.794). Relaxing the joints, particularly when the joint is designated as *hapsos*, is not loosening the cords (of the tendons), but unfastening, unfitting-as-disabling, interrupting touch. (The relevant verb is *haptô*.) Neither a specific activity nor a purely passive comportment, the relaxing unfastening of the joint, the joint's disjointing, is letting the unfastening that resides in the relation forged by a joint—and, *eo ipso*, in any relation, as that very relation—shine forth. The construal of *logos* as the gathering of discrete elements that do not touch one another, that do not share a common boundary despite the act of gathering, heeds the call for unfastening. In this, it is at variance with *muthos*, where the bonds (including the genealogical ties binding deified elements and places) are tight, and with *nous*, where the mediating linkages are absent, given its immediately intuitive, direct activity.

...

Aristotle restitutes to *logos* its body in the *Poetics*, where *arthron* reappears in the enumeration of parts of speech. Listing "the components of diction," *lexeôs . . . mere*, he includes *arthron* (*Po.* 1456b20)[40] alongside syllables, nouns, verbs, connectors, and so on. The Aristotelian definition of *arthron* is provided soon thereafter in book 20 of the *Poetics*: it is "a non-signifying sound [*phônê asêmos*] which indicates the beginning, the end, or the division of speech [*logou*]" (1457a5–6).[41] A sound bereft of meaning—a non-signifying sound—is a necessary precondition for signification. In its absence, it would be unclear how *logos* is divided, where it begins and where it ends. An attentive reading will reveal that the parts of *logos* associated with *arthron*—with the lexical joint—circle back to Plato's animal-*logos*. The beginning and the end are the same in Plato and Aristotle, but the middle, which is the crucial aspect of articulation, is now replaced with division, *diorismos*. Parts of speech *are* animal organs, and *arthron* is the medium of their interrelation, their simultaneous separation and conjoining.

With the restitution of a body to *logos*, Aristotle deserves to be understood as a philosophical biologist. Patrizia Laspia encapsulates the programmatic thrust of such an interpretation: "Within the Aristotelian research program, indeed at its heart—represented by the biological investigation—a highly significant place is occupied by the 'language/living body' analogy, which is the basis of Aristotelian linguistic investigation and especially of the twentieth chapter of the *Poetics*. Any reading of the so-called linguistic chapter of the *Poetics* that does not proceed simultaneously and in parallel with the biological investigation, which is the model of Aristotle's linguistic investigations, has in my opinion no foundation on principle."[42] It bears mentioning that both "linguistic investigations" and "life sciences" mean something quite different within the Aristotelian philosophical universe than they do in the twenty-first century. The "'language/living body' analogy" presupposes too much—the entire composition, organization, and structure of both. In order to approximate Aristotle's thinking, it would be advisable to start not from the analogy of the linguistic and biological *Gestalt*, but from the micro-site of the joint, the *arthron*, which they share.

To start, or to restart in this way, we ought to recall that, as I put it earlier, the joint is a *jointure* between the speech of the body and the body of speech; therefore, in itself, it is more than itself. While asemic, or non-signifying, in keeping with Aristotle's definition, *arthron* reflects the structure of the sign, pointing beyond itself, relating to other signs or to their referents. More than that, the structure of the sign is shaped by *arthron*, which is why it is reflected there. This pointing-beyond-itself is not an ideal and ultimately empty intending of the other (sign or signified); it is not, in other words, the holy grail of biosemiotics as we know it. *Arthron* is a persistently negotiated exercise in a difficult, messy, unstable articulation, whether it is set to work in the bodies of biological organisms or in the body of *logos*. The inevitable question of the model, or the original blueprint, for analogical formations (here: between the joints of *logos* and *zôon*), which on Plato's watch always abuts the eidetic sphere, is inapplicable here.

Less appropriate still is the emphasis on the primacy of one term of comparison over the other, culminating either in the idealist argument that living beings are organized like *logos* or in its materialist counterpart that, on the contrary, it is *logos* that is organized on the model of a biologically verifiable being. The signifying *function*—including the functions of bringing together or drawing apart, or, better, of bringing together in drawing apart and vice versa—should be foregrounded at the expense of ready-made systems if we are to appreciate the linkage between Aristotle's "linguistic investigations" and the "life sciences." But the function of articulation, as much as of the ideal-material signification it morphs into, is not at all simple; it functionally, constitutively undermines itself in order to fulfil its function. Hence, the differences between the biological connector (*sundesmos*) and the linguistic articulator (*arthron*), both of them mentioned by Aristotle under the heading "parts of speech": "In Aristotelian biology in fact, 'connector' is not at all synonymous with 'articulator.' The two terms have, if anything, opposite meanings, as the Arabic translator of the *Poetics* perceived with clever intuition."[43]

...

Articulation is the *is*. The being of the joint is being itself, in the form of the copula. Laspia writes: "Inside the simple proposition '*logos en dêlôn*' the same role is performed in my opinion by the so-called 'copula,' which today I would call 'predication operator' (*eimí*). Where it is 'predicated as a third element' (*De int.* 10, 19b19) and does not itself contain a determination of time—which it does not contain in necessary predication—*eimí* is, in my opinion, the principal type of Aristotelian *arthron*."[44] "In my opinion": repeated twice and acknowledged in a footnote to be also the opinion of Artur von Fragstein, a twentieth-century scholar of Aristotle. If Laspia and von Fragstein are correct, then *eimí*, the infinitive form of the verb *to be*, is a *type* of articulation, which consequently means that *arthron* is still more capacious than being, that there could be other types, no longer considered principal, which it embraces. And, assuming that the copula is a joint, the joint is a copula in a back-and-forth of gathering and separation, two-in-one and one-in-two. Ontology is, in a word, a *rheumontology*.

...

For the Heidegger of the *Beiträge*, "articulation" is a handy word for thinking the relation between the first and the other beginnings of thinking. The German *Fuge* means both "articulation," including in the sense of jointure in carpentry or welding, and the musical composition of the fugue; as a verb, *fügen* says "to assemble," "to fit together," "to join." (It doesn't escape Heidegger that an assemblage always slips away from a totalizing grasp, that jointure presupposes a disjoining, and that the donation of being is its withdrawal.) It is for this reason that, early on in the *Beiträge*, Heidegger proposes that the event, *Ereignis*, worthy of the name would be "joining a free jointure of the truth of beyng [*die freie Fuge der Wahrheit des Seyns aus diesem selbst zu fügen*]."[45] He wants his own contributions to philosophy to be like a receding tide that will prepare the coming one, its impetus and energy negatively and obliquely nourishing the event, just as preparation for a leap often involves taking a few steps *back* and then dashing *forward*. Whereas "joining a free jointure of truth" by thinking is unavoidably belated, at the end of metaphysics it is still too early to do so.

The language Heidegger strains to invent in order to facilitate the "leap" from the first to the other beginnings has been considered mystified, dense, and, importantly enough, inarticulate. Nevertheless, his concern is the rearticulation of articulation itself—in language, in being (or in beyng), in the world (or in what comes to supplant the old and tired theologico-metaphysical concept of the world). In other words, the task is to return to *logos*, to the assemblages, gatherings, and jointures it denotes, when this return is no longer viable, that is, when *logos* neither should nor can be named as such. In the place of *logos* and *legein*, *Fuge* and *fügen* step in with the acute feeling of non-fittingness and disarticulation implicit in these German articulations of *articulation*.

Heidegger admits that he still lacks the words for thinking at the suspended threshold between the first beginning and the other beginning. So, the "basic disposition" of thinking is triple—shock, restraint, and diffidence—but "the inner relation among these will be experienced only in thinking through the individual jointures [*im Durchdenken der einzelnen Fugen*] into which the grounding of the truth of beyng and the grounding of the essential occurrence of truth must array themselves. The word for the unity [*Einheit*] of these dispositions is lacking."[46]

Up to a point, the triad of the basic disposition recaptures the traditional philosophical attitudes of wonder (translated into shock), reason's self-limiting (cast as restraint), and the non-systemic, non-totalizing position (in the guise of diffidence). But the absence of "the word for the unity of these dispositions" may be a consequence of the aspect of diffidence, which Heidegger lists last, implying that there is no unity and that only "individual jointures" are at play in "the grounding of the truth of being." The *Fugen* in question would then be akin to joints that do not form their own arthro-system within a body. Heidegger's provisional definition of philosophy as "*a jointure in beings such that it is compliant to beyng and disposes to beyng its truth* [eine Fuge im Seienden als die sich dem Seyn fügende Verfügung über seine Wahrheit]"[47] confirms this near obsession with the singularity of jointure.

...

Saying "*logos*" in the twenty-first century is, at the same time, saying too much and too little. *Logos* is so naturalized, so domesticated—its semantic density notwithstanding—that it is no longer detected as foreign in the automatic spell-check of word-processing programs, nor is it italicized in many English publications. But it is a word without its world, the word of another epoch, the age of metaphysical gathering, which as Heidegger intuited, had drawn to a close *and* has stubbornly continued to linger on past its expiration date and beyond its bygone world. Agamben loads *logos* with extra conceptual luggage when he identifies "the relation and passage between nature and culture, between *phusis* and *logos*" as one of the "supreme problems" of Western culture. "This passage," Agamben continues, "is always already conceived as an *arthron*, an articulation; or rather, as a discontinuity that is also a continuity, a removal that is also a preservation (*arthron*, like *armonia*, originally derives from the language of woodworking; *armotto* signifies to conjoin, to unite, as the woodworker does with two pieces of wood)."[48] In woodworking, the passage between the two domains is an articulation of matter, which hails from the world of nature (especially and originally in its woody and wooden instantiation), and of form, which the artisan bestows on the two pieces by putting them together. Before "two pieces of wood" were wood, they were a tree, which was, in a unity of matter and form, a persistent articulation and rearticulation of itself (its branches, ramified roots, leaves, etc.: the persistence of these articulations and rearticulations is the time span of vegetal existence) and with others (fungi, bacteria, insects, water, solar energy). *Phusis* has a multitude of its own *logoi*, which should not be conflated with culture; *arthron* is not the "passage between" these two domains, but the way *logos* works, not least within *phusis*.

...

In the leap, which Heidegger tries to stimulate in his "middle" period, the body disappears—not because it is too abstract of a concept, as I have complained in the opening lines of this study, but because it invites a mechanicist approach to life and the living. "Since every living thing is organismic, i.e., bodily [*leiblich*], it is possible to take the bodily as the corporeal and then consider it mechanistically [*dieses Leibliche als Körper und den Körper mechanisch betrachten*]. . . . The question remains as to whether what can be done in such a (mechanistic) way ever leads to what, first and foremost, must be done, assuming that a fundamental relation to living beings is necessary."[49] Signaled by a shift from *Leib* to *Körper*, the conversion of a living body into a body is its transformation into a corpse, still before the moment of biological death (a signature Gnostic and Neoplatonic theme). Needless to say, the material substratum wherein life grows, decays, and metamorphoses is indissociable from certain mechanical processes and from the living body's thingly existence, its being a future corpse. The question is different; it is how Heidegger's rejection of "mechanicist" biology affects the body of *logos*, or what remains of it after the proposed reinvention of the very language of thinking.

Even as he criticizes biology for establishing a relation to living beings that is not fundamental enough, Heidegger favors an artisanal substitute for the gathering and discerning activity of *logos*. In particular, he favors jointure in the form of a hinge, the mechanical jointure of *Fuge*. This, in effect, is "the thinking work in the age of transition," *das denkerische Werk im Zeitalter des Übergangs*, which is the title of chapter 40 in the *Beiträge*[50]—a work openly acknowledging that what comes after *logos* and in its place is a forging and, perhaps, a forgery. But, if *Fuge* bears resemblance to the joints of a body, that is because both are articulations, with both sharing a mechanical underside.

Heidegger understands his own project in the *Beiträge* in terms of a "projection" of inceptual thinking, striving "to be a jointure [*Fuge*] of this thinking."[51] The event is the project of the *Beiträge*, presented as the preliminary articulation of the other beginning. The writing performatively hastens the early glimmers of what it is about. Heidegger will unfold the root-word of *Fuge* into the "threefold sense" of *Gefüge*, *Gefügung*, and *Fügung*: the rigorous makeup (*Gefüge*) of thought indicating the truth of being; the flexibility or the availability (*Gefügung*) of thinking to venture toward that truth; and the chance (*Fügung*) of the event happening, of being both dispensing itself and withdrawing.[52] This chance is all the higher, the more the formally incongruous first and second senses of *Fuge* are with each other. Rigor and flexibility, like grounding and leaping, are the opposites that require the right approach for their articulation, notably the articulation of articulation itself, whether it is a constructed or an organismic joint. The secret of the right approach is not so much in balancing and moderating the extremes, but in activating the one through the other without the fear of undermining each and rendering the whole wherein they participate vulnerable. Only in this self-disabling enablement does the jointure function well. (As always, Heidegger is more Hegelian than he thinks he is.)

The eventfulness of the event, Heidegger insists, hinges on jointures without a system—a shibboleth for his anti-Hegelianism. "Jointure," he writes, "is something essentially other than a 'system' [*Die Fuge ist etwas wesentlich anderes als ein 'System'*]. 'Systems' are only possible and, in the end, necessary only in the realm of the history of answers to the guiding question."[53] His *Fuge* is a *reworked logos*, holding on to questions without, or prior to, answers in a reflection on fundamental life without organisms, without organismic bodies and their quasi-mechanical properties, but with finite existence and death. The thread of rejecting the actual in favor of the possible winds back to Heidegger's *Being and Time*, where the entire existential analytic of Dasein draws support from the primacy of possibility, which is (the work's phenomenological orientation and attention to being-in-the-world notwithstanding) a disembodying factor. In the context of our concerns, a simple question interferes with the answerless question Heidegger pursues: How is a leap (*Sprung*) possible without a body and, above all, without joints?

On Hips and Shoulders.

The Ball-and-Socket Joints, or Freedom and Constriction

Although the joints of both hips and shoulders are, like those of knees and elbows, synovial (with a cavity, which affords freedom of movement), they are not hinge joints. Instead, they are of the ball-and-socket variety (enarthroses), adding rotation to the range of available movements. The shoulder joint, also called the glenohumeral joint, is a polyaxial one, permitting more freedom of movement to the arm than the hip joint, which must be able to carry the weight of the body, can give to the leg.[54] There is, therefore, a structural and functional equivalence between hip and shoulder joints, where the limbs are articulated with the trunk, but this equivalence is incomplete because of a greater need for stability at the hip.[55]

Shoulders can be load-bearing as well, carrying a burden that modifies the body and its jointed architecture. Far from a merely alien mass, whatever is carried on one's shoulders (an object, another person, or, for the population of any given country—national debt, the memory of past genocides, colonization, etc.) becomes a vertical extension of the body, temporary and detachable as it may be. The act of bearing such a burden transforms the shoulders into the second hips, which means that shoulder joints need to be stabilized on the model of their counterparts at the hip, at the expense of the arms' freedom of movement. The shoulders become support structures for things stacked up vertically in relation to the body, their weight potentially as heavy as the entire world.

The idiom "to carry the weight of the world on one's shoulders" is telling, particularly when associated with the mythical figure of the Greek Titan Atlas, who upholds the celestial sphere. The world as such has no physical weight; it is a metaphysical concept, referring to the totality of finite, temporal existence. To carry the weight of the world is to bear the heavy burden of responsibility for it, responsibility even for those things you are not guilty of, according to the conventional idea of intentionality and the juridical construal of culpability. To shoulder the weight of the globe—be it terrestrial or celestial, as in the case of Atlas—is a task at once physical and metaphysical. The bearer must furnish an objective foundation for the order of being and become a pillar responsible for keeping this order in place, not letting it crumble. Globalization has been steaming ahead without this global responsibility ("corporate responsibility" is a fig leaf barely covering such shame), without anyone or anything shouldering the weight of the globe.

The oldest surviving statue of Atlas, the second century C.E. *Farnese Atlas*, shows the Titan contorted at the joints as he sustains the celestial globe on his shoulders. Kneeling with the right knee on the ground, the left knee bent uncomfortably, his head is rotated to the right, while both arms bent at the elbows are stretched upward, so as to secure the globe, resting on his immobilized shoulders. For having sided with the

Titans in the war against the Olympians, at the end of the standoff, Atlas is punished by Zeus, who condemns him to hold up the sky at the westernmost edge of the known world: "And Atlas through hard constraint upholds the wide heaven with unwearying head and arms, standing at the borders of the earth [*peirasin en gaiês*]" (*Hes. Th.* 515–20). The "hard constraint" is both that of divine decree and of fate (*moira*), invoked in the next line of Hesiod's text, "the fate meted out to him by the wise Zeus [*oi moiran edassato mêtieta Zeus*]" (521), and that of the disabling stabilization of the shoulder joint, transformed into a second set of hips. The flexibility and the capacity for axial rotations of the glenohumeral joint are sacrificed to this other, punitive function. The joint is no longer a joint when—hardened, densified, and stabilized—it merges with the skeletal system.

...

In his influential essay "On the Shoulders of Giants," Umberto Eco speaks very little, if at all, about either shoulders or shoulder joints. He fully assumes the metaphorical nature of the expression, which he deploys to outline a sharp contrast between the ancient or medieval and modern relation to innovation. "In the Middle Ages," he writes, "people assumed that the truth of things lay in the extent to which they were backed up by an earlier authority." Conversely, "any thinkers of our day (not to mention any poets, novelists, or painters) who want to be taken seriously must somehow show that they are saying something different from their immediate predecessors, or if they are not doing so, they must pretend that they are."[56] With Stoic epistemology in the backdrop of the medieval attitude, the dividing line is clear enough—the ideal of philosophical and artistic production before the advent of modernity is that of continuity, whereas the modern ideal is a rupture and a wholly new beginning. Eco focuses on the giants (and the dwarfs) to the detriment of the shoulders that appear in his title; however, it is the shoulders that problematize the black-and-white contrast between the premodern and modern attitudes. As the statement by Bernard of Chartres, quoted by John of Salisbury, who is in turn quoted by Eco (what better proof of "standing on the shoulders of giants" than this citational chain?) intimates, the continuity of the stance conceals a rupture: "Bernard of Chartres used to say that we are like dwarfs standing on the shoulders of giants [*nos esse quasi nanos gigantium humeris insidentes*], and so we can see farther than they, not because of our sharper sight or greater stature but because we have been raised higher by their great size."[57] The incremental increase of height inaugurates a different vision, allowing those who have climbed up on the shoulders of giants to see further and to see better. The shoulders of tradition perpetually become its hips, exchanging the limited creative freedom they wielded for the role of stabilization structures with respect to future generations. Finally (though this is not a development admitting of any teleological finality), these constantly mutating shoulders-hips are the joints between the giants and the dwarfs, the greater and the lesser, the lesser who become greater than the greats by adding their nano-bodies and nano-thoughts to the current peaks of the traditional corpus.

...

With higher degrees of freedom, substantial precariousness skyrockets. As an anatomy textbook has it, the glenohumeral joint "may well be the most mobile . . . in the body," and as such, it "makes contact with only about one-third of the near-spherical head of the humerus. It follows, therefore, that bone structure contributes little to the stability of the glenohumeral joint, and a forceful blow to the shoulder is likely to cause joint separation."[58] The mobility of the joint holds the seeds of its demise.

In the tragic case of the Shoah survivor Jean Améry, torture in Auschwitz did not imply "a forceful blow to the shoulder," but suspension from a ceiling hook by his arms tied behind his back. The blows that preceded this horrible moment were many, but the first one, the first blow meant a breakdown of basic trust in the world. Améry writes: "I don't know if the person who is beaten by the police loses human dignity. Yet I am certain that with the very first blow that descends on him he loses something we will perhaps temporarily call 'trust in the world.'"[59] Before joints come on stage, a disjoining happens; the articulation of "written or unwritten social contracts" that hold together without fusing the one and the many crumbles. The violence of torture (and of rape, equally mentioned by Améry) strikes, through the body of the tortured or the raped, at the very social joints that enliven the notion of coexistence, and thus of existence as such.

The breaking of social joints is followed in quick succession by the dislocation of Améry's shoulder joints:

> In the bunker there hung from the vaulted ceiling a chain that above ran into a roll. At its bottom end it bore a heavy, broadly curved iron hook. I was led to the instrument. The hook gripped into the shackle that held my hands together behind my back. Then I was raised with the chain until I hung about a meter over the floor. In such a position, or rather, when hanging this way, with your hands behind your back, for a short time you can hold at a half-oblique through muscular force. During these few minutes, when you are already expending your utmost strength, when sweat has already appeared on your forehead and lips, and you are breathing in gasps, you will

> not answer any questions. Accomplices? Addresses? Meeting places? You hardly hear it. All your life is gathered in a single, limited area of the body, the shoulder joints, and it does not react; for it exhausts itself completely in the expenditure of energy. But this cannot last long, even with people who have a strong physical constitution. As for me, I had to give up rather quickly. And now there was a crackling and splintering in my shoulders that my body has not forgotten until this hour. The balls sprang from their sockets. My own body weight caused luxation; I fell into a void and now hung by my dislocated arms, which had been torn high from behind and were now twisted over my head.[60]

The immobilization of Améry's body on the hook, from which he was suspended by his hands, shackled behind his back, is, by the same token, a paralysis of his mind; he is unable to answer the interrogator's questions, even if he wants to. This unsustainable, untenable *position* (a word he retracts in favor of "hanging this way") of Améry's body between the ceiling and the floor transfigures all of it into a joint, an articulation of the in-between. For a brief moment, his "life is gathered in a single, limited area of the body, the shoulder joints," as though in a vain effort to live up to such a transfiguration. The concentration of vitality in the joints is short-lived: they crackle and splinter, the ball and the socket of the shoulder joint separating. Ball *or* socket; the in-between is disjointed, no longer situated between determinate limits. Hence, "the void," the same void, into which torture plugs its evil logic as effectively as—albeit by means other than—the discerning knife of Plato's carver and Zhuang Zhou's cook.

Writing decades after the act of torture he underwent, Améry finds himself in the traumatized and impassible present of torture, of the disarticulated shoulder joints and dislocated arms: "Torture has an indelible character. Whoever was tortured, stays tortured."[61] And, by way of speculatively revisiting this ever-present traumatic non-experience, he observes how the body's own weight, its sheer materiality, did the work of torture: "My own body weight caused luxation." At the opposite end of the first blow, which comes from the outside shattering one's trust in the world, the hanging body becomes its own torturer.

In the eighteenth-century study of the organism from the perspective of "natural theology," William Paley examines the ligaments keeping the two parts of the ball-and-socket joint together. "It is hardly indeed imaginable," he quips, "how great a force is necessary, even to stretch, still more to break, this ligament; yet so flexible is it, as to oppose no impediment to the suppleness of the joint."[62] Améry knows full well what that great force is, namely gravity pulling the body in an unnatural and unsustainable, suspended position down to earth.

...

On the one hand, excessive rigidity is imposed on the shoulder joints. Immobilized, they support the vertical extension of the body, which finds its continuation in the burden it shoulders. On the other hand, bearing the burden of the body itself, of which they are part, shoulder joints are disjointed: the ball of the glenohumeral enarthrosis comes out of its socket. The destruction of the joint happens as a result of the excesses of separation *and* fusion. Whether loosening or hardening too much, the joint ceases to do what it is meant to do. Absolute freedom and unconditional openness (hospitality?) of the joint can be terrible: a dismemberment of the body.

...

Before he receives the first blow, Améry recounts what is unmistakably a liberal-bourgeois version of the relation to his own body and the laws governing its relations to the bodies of others. "An element of trust in the world, and, in our context, what is solely relevant, is the certainty that by reason of written or unwritten social contracts the other person will spare me—more precisely stated, that he will respect my physical, and with it also my metaphysical, being. The boundaries of my body are also the boundaries of my self. My skin surface shields me against the external world. If I am to have trust, I must feel on it only what I *want* to feel."[63] Yet, skin both shields, drawing the boundaries of the body and the self, and, for better or for worse, exposes this body, indistinguishable from the self, to the outside world. Being in the world means that I cannot feel only what I want to feel on my skin and throughout the perimeter of my "physical" and "metaphysical" being. Rather than an either/or situation, the blows and the torture they participate in are the extreme consequences of this vital openness, or the openedness, of the body.

The body, here as elsewhere, is Améry's biological organism, as much as the social body, persistently adumbrated in interactions with others. The dislocation of the shoulder joints is tied to the breaking apart of the social bond. Words no longer provide the articulatory mediation between the torturer and the tortured; questions morph into yet another instrument of torture. The torturer-other is not another person, but the source of unspeakable pain: "For the tortured, the torturer is solely the other, and here he will be regarded as such. Who were the others, who pulled me up by my dislocated arms and punished my dangling body with the horsewhip?"[64] Just as the joint is damaged by excessive rigidity or excessive laxity, so the freedom and obligation that normally articulate social relations are polarized in torture. Claimed by the torturer, freedom is the freedom to inflict anything onto the tortured and, by means of this unlimited exercise, to take away their freedom, well-being, and lives. Obligation is the heavy onus put on the tortured, to suffer, including from the fact, or the facticity, of their own embodiment.

In addition to the rupturing of the social bond and of shoulder joints, the order of time breaks down. If past, present, and future are the joints of time (essentially, as we will see in a little while, every moment is such a joint, both continuous and discontinuous), then the trauma of torture, which imprisons the tortured in an unending present, destroys the joints of time. "It still is not over," Améry laments. "Twenty-two years later I am still dangling over the ground by dislocated arms, panting, and accusing myself."[65] The present cut loose from the past and from the future is the atemporal state of trauma. While according to calendar time torture happened in the past, for the tortured that past never ends, never really passes; it is present, it is in the present, regardless of the twenty-two years that have elapsed since then. In its temporal or atemporal being, trauma is the rigidity of what is unsurpassable and the dissociation of the present from other modalities of time. It disarticulates time itself. And, the other way around, the standard of atemporal metaphysical being is trauma hypostatized and idealized, raised to the status of the one and only truth.

...

Shoulders can be free when you do not treat them like second hips. When you stand with others shoulder-to-shoulder, facing a common task for the good of all, the outlines of freedom and equality emerge on the horizon of such a community. Instead of latching onto a prosthetic body in a vertical extension, the shoulder joint assembles itself with other such joints horizontally. The risk is that, gathering shoulder-to-shoulder, a group would unite *against* the other deemed to be an enemy, not *for* the sake of seeking and actualizing the good. More accurately put, it could mobilize the *for* for the sake of the *against*. The political joint par excellence! (What would a stance hip-to-hip, rather than shoulder-to-shoulder, amount to?)

...

What is it that visually unites hip and shoulder joints, which are functionally similar but quite distant from each other in the human body? As I pored over this question, I came across a political artifact, almost universally associated with the highest echelons of power and the military: the sash. A large band, draped around one shoulder, descending to the opposite hip and back up (or sometimes tied around the waist), the sash is an emblem of authority and of knighthood, currently also adopted by presidents around the world. As I suspected, the sash boasts a long history. Given the origins of the word itself (derived from the Arabic شَاش, *shash*, or muslin cloth), this ceremonial ribbon is traceable to the Muslim world, where it initially referred to the band used for the making of a turban.[66] In medieval Castile, the sash was featured in what Jesús Rodríguez-Velasco calls "the poetics of *ordo*," the extra- or paralegal institution and staging of social peace, moderating the upheavals built into the institution of knighthood.[67]

The current ceremonial significance of the sash harkens back to its symbolic reference to peace, itself linked, as Rodríguez-Velasco aptly puts it, to pacification.[68] Superimposed onto the body of the sovereign figure, such as a president, the sash integrates parts of this body that are not only directly unrelated to each other, but also indirectly opposed: for instance, the right shoulder and the left hip. The real import of this integration is that the individual body of the sovereign, even when not a monarch, is a miniature version of the entire body politic. Although it connects the opposite shoulder and hip in a temporary and superficial manner, the sash signals the end of arthro-anarchy, of the non- or anti-systemic arrangement of the joints, and of the freedom (of movement) that the enarthroses embody. Cast over the joints that activate both the arms and the legs, it "covers" the totality of physical and political actions. Were this bond between the shoulders and the hips permanent, it would have immobilized the body of the sovereign and, by implication, paralyzed a fully integrated and entirely pacified body politic.

In the Castilian context, the sash was so prominent that in 1332, King Alfonso XI founded an order of the Knights of the Sash (*de la Banda*)[69] in Vitoria-Gasteiz, on the occasion of incorporating the province of Álava, now a part of the Basque Country, into the kingdom of Castile. From a common name for the ceremonial piece, the sash, worn diagonally from the right shoulder to the waist on the left, was converted into the proper name of an order. The elite force of the Knights of the Sash operated in such a way that none of its inductees would be individuated, standing out from the rest. In extant historical documents, "the references allude to the group in general, and they never refer to the individual knights who may have been members of the Sash. The first mention is quite generic and praises the Sash."[70] The cohesiveness of the Knights of the Sash as a military formation was thus reflected in the group's metonymic naming after the band, spanning the shoulder and hip joints equally denied their individuality.

...

Order: *arthron*: *rtá*. Émile Benveniste's foray into the etymology of the word "order" reveals that the Greek precursor of the term is *harmonia*, which itself goes back to the Sanskrit *rtá* (the source of, among other words, "right").[71] *Rtá* conveys the fittingness of things in their mutual support and articulation among themselves. It is the ordering, which an order (including a military or a knightly order) expresses, substantivizes, rigidifies, and ultimately extinguishes. Articulations put the dynamic harmony of *rtá* into practice—hence the significance of *arthron*, all too often eclipsed by *harmonia*, the other etymological descendant of *rtá*. Together with *logos* and *jiê*, *rtá* is the articulation of articulation, the jointure of joints, and the root of art.

...

About half a century before Alfonso XI founded the knightly order *de la Banda* in Castile, Rabbi Moses de León and his disciples had been completing the manuscript of the *Zohar* (*Brilliance*), the centerpiece of medieval Jewish Kabbalah.[72] Analogous to other medieval Abrahamic mysticisms—notably, the works of Ibn ʿArabī and Hildegard von Bingen—the *Zohar* explores, in minute details, a theo-anatomy, that is, the organization of the divine body from the unknowable celestial regions of God's head all the way down to earth. The flows of emanations (*sefirot*), cascading from the highest infinity (*ein-sof*) or crown (*keter*), suggest a hydraulic model of divine energies, but, in a denser state, the *sefirot* are valves that regulate and channel these flows. Viewed anatomically, they are the joints, across which the body of God assembles itself.

Among the lowest *sefirot*, there are the two divine "thighs" connected through hip joints to the torso: eternity or victory (*netzakh*) and splendor (*hod*). Largely overlooked in kabbalistic literature, *netzakh* and *hod* are the sources of prophecy. Concerning the former, it is written: "*Netzakh Israel*, Eternity of Israel (1 Samuel 15:29) . . . This is the fourth rung from which no human prophesied until Samuel arrived" (*Zohar* 1:21b; v.

1, p. 163).[73] Israel is the alternative name of Jacob, while *netzakh* is taken in the sense of victory (*nitzakhon*)—here the victory of Jacob over the angel, with whom he wrestled in Genesis 32. Jacob must pay for his victory with the weakness of his thigh: "Then this rung was mended, for it had been weak ever since Jacob was endangered by the Prince Esau. *He touched the socket of his thigh* (Genesis 32:26). When he reached Jacob, he seized the power from that *turning of the evening* in severe Judgment" (*Zohar* 1:21b; v. 1, p. 163). But what does this have to do with prophecy?

Articulating different modalities of time outside a linear chronology, prophecy is a peculiar link between the present and the future. The prophet is a singular joint between times. Moreover, prophecy itself is a jointure between the order of time and timelessness (eternity, *netzakh*). For a brief moment, the difference between what is and what will be is erased, but this transitory erasure of time transpires *in* time, in the now, in an instant of prophetic vision or speech. So the joint is an appropriate anatomical representation of prophecy—but why the hip joint? And why single out "the socket of his thigh," damaged ("wrenched") in Jacob's skirmish with the angel?

Prophetic discourse is bereft of a firm ground in the present. It has no terrestrial support, which would sustain it; instead, it moves with the help of a damaged thigh joint—and its effect, limping—that irradiates the power of prophecy. Much in the same vein, the classical figure of the blind seer confirms the uselessness of (or even the obstruction created by) physical sight, as compared to a spiritual vision capable of beholding nothing immediately present: the seer sees the future, in part, out of this deficiency of corporeal vision. Within its medieval context, the *Zohar* attributes the deficiency of *netzakh* to its location on the left side of the divine body of *sefirot*: "*Netzakh*, Eternity, is the left thigh of Jacob. . . . Why was Jacob's thigh weakened? Because the side of impurity approached, seizing power from it" (*Zohar* 1:21b; v. 1, p.

164). Here, as in many other Judeo-Christian medieval sources, the left side is associated with the devil, with the "impurity" of demonic power, supernatural in its abilities. But from the chronological perspective, the "weakness" of the damaged left hip joint is a corollary of temporal disorder, a maladjustment of the usual succession, in which the future comes on the heels of the present. Instead, disjointing the modalities of time (and reassembling them otherwise), the future prophetically erupts in the present *sub specie aeternitatis*, under the aspect of eternity, *netzakh*.

Hod, or splendor, is the other hip joint of the sefirotic body. "Joshua prophesied from the *Hod*, *Splendor* of Moses, as is written: *Confer me-hodekha, of your splendor, upon him* (Numbers 27:20)" (*Zohar* 1:21b; v. 1, p. 164). *Hod* mirrors and counterbalances *netzhakh*. As the other hip joint, it introduces a sense of symmetry and measure, of justice and adjustment in what is intrinsically maladjusted. That is why, jointly, *netzakh* and *hod* make up a scale: "Who is *a scale*? Rabbi Shim'on said, 'As is written: *scales of equity, weights of equity* (Leviticus 19:36)" (*Zohar* 2:175b; v. 5, p. 528). Divine hip joints combine openness and closure, flexibility and stability, the flash of splendor and the endurance of eternity, the ball and the socket.[74] They compensate for the weakness of each taken singly with the pairing that revamps them into "scales"—of the present and the future, of walking on earth and in the sky.

...

Hip joints allow the body to fold, assuming the sitting position or bending forward and down. They free the bipedal animals that we are from our upright posture and form a crease between verticality and horizontality, or (as in a forward-down bend) between the ascending and the descending vectors of vertical corporeity. The work of the hip joints is that of insistence and resistance: the office jobs that ruin the backs of office workers over the long hours of sitting at a desk, on the one hand, and the sit-ins in political protests that bend the body otherwise, no longer in compliance but in defiance of the system, which exploits it. It is noteworthy that, at the hips, not this or that limb folds and unfolds, but the body as a whole assumes an intermediate position, neither standing up nor lying down. The hip enarthrosis is the hotspot of indeterminacy, where the positing and the deposing, the *thesis* and the *antithesis* or the *allothesis*, converge.

. . .

Delving into Plato's *hystera*, the cave reimagined as a womb, in *Speculum of the Other Woman*, Luce Irigaray contemplates the conditions of possibility for the production of this primal philosophical scene—and of the spectacle staged upon it. The dark cave, where the absent eidetic light finds its faint reflection in the fire illuminating the procession of moving illusions, is the space and the time of violence, of violation, of dismemberment and disarticulation. "Such an enterprise is never simple," Irigaray writes. "Here the properties of the eye, of mirrors—and indeed of spacing, of space-time, of time—are dislocated, disarticulated, disjointed, and only later brought back to the perspective-free contemplation of the truth of the Idea. Idea eternally present, postulated by the separation, the dismembering of, on the one hand, the 'amorphous' but insistent anteriority of the *hystera*, that unrepresentable origin of all forms and all morphology, and, on the other hand, the dazzling fascination of the Sun—image of the Good."[75]

The event of dislocation and disarticulation transpires in the eye, affecting physical sight as much as space and time: eidetic vision is the disordering of physical sight. To be sure, the properties of the eye are "dislocated, disarticulated, disjointed," but the cave with its "insistent anteriority" is the consistent context, the setting, the atmosphere wherein this happens. The eye socket is the cave of the eye: "Thus a bony cavernous socket encloses the eye. An inside-out socket, in this case, in which the gaze is swallowed up in a vault."[76] It is the ball-and-socket joint of the hip, though, as the closest to Plato's speculum examining the womb of existence in the feminized version of the cave, that bears the heaviest brunt of disarticulation. Just as the Sun is the enucleated eye shining in the sky (and, hence, no longer in the cave of the body, in its socket set in the skull), so the hip joint is torn apart, the ball removed from its socket in the violent disruption of its articulated structure, so as to permit the closest approximation to the world of the cave from the feigned exteriority of the eidetic gaze. The gynecology of spirit is inseparable from its rheumatology.

The "potency of the gaze," described by Irigaray, is also indissociable from the act of dismembering and disjoining, which revels in an unlimited drive to analyze. This potency is of speculation and of specula, "of mirrors. Of eyes 'like' mirrors, that are not, always already, broken and articulating the break, but rather are artificially disjointed and divided into properties offering an illusion of analysis, and addition, and multiplication, up to the highest power. The unit!"[77] The freedom of the mobile joint does not bar the possibility of disjointure; instead, it hinges on this very possibility. But when the possibility is realized "to the highest power," accompanied by the nagging feeling that it is never sufficient, that analysis has not yet been radical enough, has not gone far enough in the direction of breaking all that is down to individual properties and the smallest units, then the joint stops working. Analysis unchained, the freedom of the joint hypostatized, is death. (Hegel dedicated some of the most powerful pages of his *Phenomenology* to teasing out this insight in the "Absolute Freedom and Terror" section of the book.)

For her part, Irigaray refers to "the illusion of analysis" and the "artificially disjointed" system of ocular mirrors. Why? Because synthesis and analysis, joining together and falling apart, enfolding and unfolding, are rhythmic movements, and more than anything, it is this vital rhythm that the Platonic power disrupts. The joint encrypts the rhythmicality of jointure *and* non-artificial disjointure. There is no such thing as analysis in the absence of its articulation with synthesis.

The either/or choice (itself gravitating toward a pure, purified analysis) is between the breaking of the joint and its immobilization, particularly at the hip or at the thigh. Once made, such a choice can never let the joint work, whatever the extreme that has been chosen. The unfreedom of the cave immobilizes the neck and the thighs: "Chained by the neck and thighs, they [the prisoners] are fixed with their heads and genitals facing *front, opposite*—which in Socrates' tale, is the direction toward the back of the cave. The cave is the representation of something always already there, of the original matrix/womb which these men cannot represent since they are held down by chains that prevent them from turning their heads or their genitals toward the daylight."[78]

The head and the genitals—the two ends of the vertical poles of the body and the psyche, or, in a word, of ancient psychophysiology—are held in the same (seated) position by the medial and atlantoaxial joints, as well as the enarthrosis, that become bone-like owing to the chains that hold them down. They are deprived of the capacity to turn, which is a matter of revolution, cosmic and political, psychic and physical, the rotation that, in a vertebrate body, is the function of the ball-and-socket and the pivot joints. From the opposite direction, a violent disjointure that breaks every terrestrial articulation thwarts revolutionary motions. It twists the imprisoned body-and-soul out of its chains on the condition that this psychophysiological cluster be left behind, happily discarded as an obstacle on the path of "perspective-free contemplation."

Arthro-Psychophysiology.

Joints in the Composition of the Body and the Soul

The task of reexamining the body from the vantage point of the joints is not easy, nor can it be accomplished in a hurry. For one thing, "the body" is incoherent without its open-ended self-articulation according to the genetic program and a conjunction of external conditions (environmental, cultural, political). For another, assuming that the Cartesian body/mind split has been overcome, the jointure in question is not only genetic and environmental, but also psychophysical, or, in another discursive register, psychosomatic. The articulated body, then, is to be elucidated in conjunction with the psychic sphere and *its* articulations, spatial as much as cognitive and vocal.

When Empedocles imagines the emergence of bodies, he starts with their disjointed state, reflecting at the level of organs the primordial chaos (of elements, or roots) prior to the formation of the cosmic whole: "Here many heads sprang up [*eblastêsan*] without necks, bare arms were wandering without shoulders, and eyes without foreheads strayed singly" (Fr. 57 [50]).[79] The limbs and other organs spring up "here," out of the earth, just like the shoots of plants do. They are an extension of geo-corporeality, among other elemental roots that bring them into being. Unlike plants, though, they are unattached either to the earth, which bears them, or to each other: arms are bare because they lack the joints, which would connect them to shoulders, and so on. As a result, Empedocles postulates the primordial errancy of body parts, wandering and straying in their disorganized, indeterminate, forlorn, negatively free state.

The next stage in the generation of bodies is the haphazard fusion of organs: "But as god mingled further with god, they fell together as they chanced to meet each other, and many others in addition to these were constantly arising" (Fr. 59 [51]).[80] The divine (*daimôn*) dimension, to which the analogy alludes, is that of a perfect proportion of the four elements (earth, air, fire, and water), which grants a long-lasting life to the being, in which the elemental roots are appropriately assembled. Their immoderate fusion at the second stage of body formation is still incompatible with proportionality. Relative to the excessive detachment and errancy of the first stage, it swings to the other extreme, producing unviable composite creatures, such as "man-faced bulls" "and again bull-headed men" (Fr. 61 [52]).[81]

Total disjointure and indiscriminate fusion are counterbalanced by love, which grants organic existence viability by articulating its parts in what is one of the earliest mentions of *arthron*, "joint," in Greek texts. Aristotle reports in *De anima* (430a28) that "as Empedocles said that 'where heads of many creatures come to birth without necks,' they are then put together by love [*suntithesthai tê Philias*]." The word *suntithesthai* ("put together," "synthetized") is Aristotle's; it is not a part of the cited Empedocles passage. Instead, the pre-Socratic speaks of "love . . .

inborn in mortal joints [*Philotês . . . thnêtoisi nomizetai emphutos arthrois*]" (Fr. 17).[82] "Mortal joints," *thnêtoisi arthrois*, are the living bodies themselves, the bodies that owe their consolidation, their gathering into coherent entities, to the unifying power of love. The ancient Greek metonymy of joints standing in for limbs and other organs is here extended to the entire body as a token of acknowledgment that the body becomes what it is through the activity of the joint, setting love to work in mortal flesh.[83]

As for love, its association with the joint complicates considerably the story Empedocles tells about its antithetical relation to strife. On the face of it, "the elements are continually subject to an alternate change, at one time mixed together [*sugkrinomena*] by love, at another separated by strife."[84] Yet, the alternate effects of love and strife, united in a cycle (*kuklos*), indicate that theirs is not a sheer stand-off (which would be an unbalanced relation languishing in the long shadow of strife, of unrestricted analysis and dissociation) but a more intricate sort of dance. Empedocles gives an indication of this in the extant opening phrase of his *Physica*, "A twofold tale I shall tell [*dipl' ereô*]" (Fr. 17 [8]),[85] echoing the two paths Parmenides charts in his poem, one of which turns out to be a non-path, an aporetic way. The opening, too, is a textual joint (and in more senses than one). Whereas the cyclical alternations of love and strife combine these apparently antithetical forces in time, the joint is a primarily spatial, though also temporal, combination of the two. The love that is "inborn in mortal joints" must have something of strife in it, or at least it must cohabit with its opposite in the same material formation defined by the simultaneity of bringing elements together and drawing them apart. The body "as a whole" is a broken totality, assembled with the help of love-strife joints. Despite its aspiration to preserve beings, to put or to keep them together, making them the beings that they are, love is fractured and finite, the memory and anticipation of loss.

...

From within the body, joints signal how the body is uncontainable in itself, how meaningless it is without connections to other bodies, to the elements, to the world. They conjoin and disjoin existence in itself and with the other. Standing in for organs and the entire organic corporeity, joints impart their non-identity to the fractured wholes of which they are parts and which they come to represent. Better than "connective tissues," they epitomize the bio-logic of sociality. Joints connect and disconnect in the intermediate and intermittent space and time of relations.

...

Lest we deem the Empedocles fragments about disjointed and fused organs a fanciful account of evolution, we should pay close attention to an infant's *experience* of the body. In line with object-relations theory and developmental psychoanalysis (Sándor Ferenczi, Melanie Klein, Donald Winnicott), a newborn is a bundle of sensations without an integrated body sense. Psychologically mapping and, bit by bit, putting the body together is a long and complicated story. Although Freud himself does not apply his theory of cathexis (*Besetzung*: a displaceable and variable quantity of psychic energy, either freely circulating or bound to an object, rendering it significant)[86] to this story, it follows from the theory of psychoanalysis that initially separate organs and ultimately the body "as a whole" need to be cathected to attain their significance and, indeed, to become significant aspects of what or who I am. More than that, cathexes may be viewed as psychic *and* as psychosomatic joints between the body and the conscious/unconscious mind. At times mobile (free), at other times static (bound), they are responsible for the dynamic nature of psychodynamic psychology.

With respect to separate organs prior to the ever so provisional integration of the body into a coherent whole, the distinction between one's own organs and those of others does not yet hold. Klein explains the phenomena of identification and libidinal attachment starting from a relation to the maternal breast:

> The ego comes to a realization of its love for a good object, a whole object and in addition a real object, together with an overwhelming feeling of guilt towards it. Full identification with the object based on libidinal attachment, first to the breast, then to the whole person, goes hand in hand with anxiety (of its disintegration), with guilt and remorse, with a sense of responsibility for preserving it intact against persecutors and the id, and with sadness relating to expectation of the impending loss of it. These emotions, whether conscious or unconscious, are in my view among the essential and fundamental elements of the feelings we call love.[87]

Before identification with the other, the infant identifies with the breast—a "good" object to the extent that it is available to satisfy hunger, though it can easily revert to a "bad" object when it is withdrawn and no longer available. It is this withdrawal, or the mere possibility thereof, that provokes anxiety and gives a premonition of the object's disintegration, its identity not being guaranteed. The breast is a joint in the ancient Greek sense of *arthron*, representing a body member, an organ, and finally the entire sphere of corporeality. Psychologically, too, it is a joint that animates psychic life through the contradictory but intertwined processes of libidinal attachment and detachment (disintegration, loss), which means that, regardless of the efforts and energy poured into self-integration, the self is never whole. As in Empedocles, Kleinian love is a connection irremediably splintered, a *connecting connection*, which is in effect thanks to and across the disconnects it can neither fully bridge nor erase. "Inborn in mortal joints," to reiterate the phrase of Empedocles, Kleinian love is, likewise, at home in the heart of finitude.

In feminist scholarship, Klein has been often criticized for her essentialism and for universally assigning the mother role to women. That said, the good object does not have to be a breast; it may as well be a baby bottle, a biberon, without, at the same time, nullifying the loving attachment foregrounded by Klein. Here, Winnicott's "transitional objects" come to mind. Such objects, according to Winnicott, "are not part of the infant's body yet are not fully recognized as belonging to external reality."[88] They are, in other words, the joints between interiority and exteriority, between natural and artificial domains, between oneself and the other. "I have introduced the terms 'transitional object' and 'transitional phenomena,'" Winnicott writes, "for designation of the intermediate area of experience, between the thumb and the teddy bear, between the oral erotism and true object relationship, between primary creative activity and the projection of what has already been introjected, between primary unawareness of indebtedness and the acknowledgement of indebtedness."[89]

Nonetheless, with joints things are more complicated than they first look. Before transitional objects and phenomena play their part, the thumb is *already* transitional, a substitute for the breast or the bottle: "The thumb represents the breast or bottle which the anxious or lonely infant needs to keep in his mouth or just outside it."[90] The very formulation "for the breast or the bottle" undoes the distinction between an organ and a manufactured object. The infant receives them as one and the same thing, based on their function in the intake of nourishment, but a function that is a priori non-indifferent, that is saturated with desire, attraction, love. This gives a very peculiar twist to the notion of transition and "transitional": contrary to what Winnicott seems to believe, transitional phenomena are not links in a teleological chain, leading up to the establishment of a "true object relationship." There are only transitions within transitions within transitions . . . , from the "beginning" of the sexually charged practice of feeding to the "end" of a mature relation, neither of which is free from transitional dynamics, that is, the operations of psychophysical joints, where the distinctions between fetishes and cathexes become incredibly blurry.

Experience as such is a transitional, intermediate process, oscillating between projection and introjection, the recognition and non-recognition of exteriority as truly exterior, discrete objects (which, as objects, are always part objects, outcomes of splitting and projection in a fantasy that *actually* splits the world into a conjunction of well-delimited entities) and flowing processes. The illusion, not least of the analytic variety, is that the transition enacted by a transitional object is at some point in time complete in psychological development which proceeds along an average trajectory—not pathologically debilitated, not plagued by fixations and traumas. Such an illusion is analogous to the image of a healthy vertebrate body without joints, or with the joints absorbed into the bones, between which they have been slotted. The joints, on the contrary, are the fulcra of a mobile vertebrate body, and libidinal joints (cathexes, part objects, transitional objects) are equally essential to the psychic body. To dissolve cathexes in libidinal fluxes, as Deleuze and Guattari recommend while reducing object-relations and psychosomatic joints to machine assemblages, or to transition away from transitional phenomena, as Winnicott's developmental psychology prescribes, is to disjoint the psyche, in one stroke liberating and paralyzing it.

...

Arthralgia, or pain of the joints, comes in many varieties. It may result from mechanical injuries (hitting or twisting the joint) or from chronic, debilitating conditions, such as arthritis and osteoarthritis. In many cases, arthralgia is accompanied by joint inflammation and counterintuitive clinical evidence. In degenerative osteoarthritis, unlike in other kinds of arthritis, "pain may be reduced during walking, and pain may be particularly severe during rest at night when the joint is immobile."[91] Pain at the sites of connection and disconnection, at the internally divided gathering points of the body, is so deep, nearly unbearable, because it is the pain of *bodying*, of the becoming-body of the body, and of its unbecoming. What about arthralgia in the bodies of *logos*, of psyche, of society, of a world? What kinds of frictions and inflammations at the joints, what kinds of injured transitions and experiences, incite it? Is the arthritic pain of a world and of a word lessened with movement, increasing pressure on the joints, or does it become unbearable when they are forced out of their temporary immobility? Is it a telltale sign of the world (and the word, to boot) growing old, wearing off at its joints, which is why all kinds of prosthetic articulations, drawn from information technology, come to supplant them?

...

Since his earliest writings, such as the 1886 "Paris Report," Freud had treated cases of arthralgia as clinical manifestations of hysteria, both male and female. In his studies with Charcot, he discussed the "somatic signs" of hysteria, including "hysterical paralyses and arthralgias" (*SE* 1: 11–12). This was not a sophisticated theoretical trick of dismissing pain in the joints as *merely* psychosomatic, that is, felt in the body without any underlying physical or physiological foundation. As Freud recognizes in his 1888 paper on hysteria, "'local hysteria' may accompany local illnesses of individual organs; a joint which is really fungal can become the seat of a hysterical arthralgia; a stomach with catarrhal affection can give rise to hysterical vomiting" (*SE* 1: 53). Here, an organ comes into the focus of a patient's attention, often, as Freud observes, for reasons of already being afflicted with an illness, and *by virtue of this hyperattention* the patient develops hysterical symptomatology. Hysteria produces psychosomatic effects not because the affliction is a purely imagined one, but rather because something goes wrong with the relation of the body and the mind—for instance, an overinvestment of libidinal energy in what Freud will later term *the binding of cathexes* to a given body part or organ. It is for this reason that his clinical recommendation to treating physicians is to discourage the already existing excess of attention: "One must guard against exhibiting too clearly one's interest as a physician in slight hysterical symptoms and so encouraging them" (*SE* 1: 54).

Differently put, psychosomatic disorders offer us a unique point of access to the joints connecting (and disconnecting) the mind and the body, there where these are jarring, causing frictions and inflammations that interfere with a person's everyday life.[92] When do psychosomatic joints work well? As a rule, when one is neither hypersensitized nor desensitized to the basic experience of embodiment. There is a fairly wide spectrum between these two extremes, and certain physico-spiritual exercises, such as practices of meditation or breathing, may draw attention to the experience of embodiment without provoking a hysterical or neurasthenic reaction. But outside a persistent training routine, eruptions of hyperattention to a body part, bordering on fixation, are likely to be unsettling, while responding to a prior and still ongoing unsettlement, irrespective of its etiology. The body-psyche nexus is then revealed *negatively*, in an event of its *disjointure*.

Freud returns to the issue of arthralgia, emphasizing this compromised connection, in his writings on hysteria: "If a slight injury to a joint is gradually followed by a severe arthralgia, no doubt the process involves a psychical element, viz. a concentration of attention on the injured part, which intensifies the excitability of the nerve tracts concerned. But this can hardly be expressed by saying that the hyperalgia has been caused by ideas" (*SE* 2: 190). The concentration of attention binds (cathects) large quantities of free libidinal energy to the object of that concentration—here, a slightly injured joint, which consequently corresponds to a disproportionately large knot of cathexes. Excitability and sensitivity then increase at crucial, hyper-cathected spots.

Still with regard to the same example of local hysteria at the joints, Freud notes that "whereas in normal people a quantity of excitation, after cathecting a sensory path, always leaves it again, this is not so in these cases. That quantity, moreover, not only remains behind but is constantly increased by the influx of fresh excitations. A slight injury to a joint thus leads to arthralgia" (*SE* 2: 241). In addition to a disproportionate cathexis, taking the form of undying attention, the psychosomatic knot keeps growing, accumulating more and more bound libidinal energy at the joint. Normally, Freud avers, excitation ebbs and flows—"after cathecting a sensory path," a quantum of energy "leaves it again"—but, in local hysteria, bound quanta linger on and snowball with fresh additions of the same. This implies psychological indigestibility, a stoppage in the metabolism of libidinal energy with its rhythms of binding, freeing, and rebinding. Such indigestibility prepares the ground for neuroses and, in the last instance, for trauma, which is the experience or non-experience that does not pass, that does not become the past. In our terms, it means that psychic and psychosomatic joints do not work as they should: that they are immobilized and rigidified. Their rigidity is temporal more than spatial, in that the instant "after" the cathexis of a sensory path never arrives, or arrives with a huge delay. Unclenching is not followed by clenching at the site of an abnormal cathexis. The joint is out of joint, because it is stuck in itself.

...

Reverting to Greek, it is possible to express a subtle shift in the workings of joints, inexpressible in English. Much depends on the joint's designation as *arthron* or *hapsos*. The fittingness that pertains to *arthron* is an articulation of two mutually opposed and sometimes mutually undermining gestures: clenching and release, release in clenching and clenching in release. *Hapsos* underscores the grasping, or the fastening, of an articulatory nexus (as a reminder: *haptô* means "I fasten"). Cathexes, as the joints of the psyche, seem to fall on the side of *hapsos*, in that they bind quanta of the otherwise free-flowing libidinal energy. But the hyperbolic movement of this fastening contributes to the formation of psychological complexes, fixations, neurosis, and traumas. What has been bound must be unbound for attention to be modulated, for psychic and psychosomatic joints to keep moving within determinate boundaries (while others, necessarily more stable, such as psychic sutures or fused articulations, stay in place). The other extreme is similarly damaging. Eschewing any commitments, anchors, and fastening lines, free-flowing currents of libidinal energy imply absolute indifference, apathy, and such a complete absence of attention that even the term "distraction" would be inappropriate to describe this condition.

...

Faced with psychosomatic manifestations, it is exceptionally difficult to distinguish physical illness *proper* from bodily reactions to psychological issues that fail to find another outlet. In reports of clinical cases featuring his pediatric patients, Winnicott details his struggle to do just that in the case of arthralgias, which are typically ascribed to underlying pathogenic or physiological causes, such as chorea or a bacterially induced "rheumatic fever." This work involves a very precise and delicate operation on the joints of the body and the psyche, separating them when it comes to disease etiology and uniting them when it comes to symptomatology. This work on the joint is itself an act of jointure, at the same time detaching and reattaching psychosomatic assemblages along the points of their contact.

At the L.C.C. Rheumatism Clinic in London, Winnicott devised a system aimed at providing more accurate diagnoses. "I soon learned," he reminisces, "to put patients into one of five categories, and I put the notes in coloured folders so as to make sure that mistakes in diagnosis would become evident.

> *Orange*. Past or present rheumatic carditis already evident and beyond doubt.
>
> *Pink*. Probable rheumatic disease but no definite carditis found.
>
> *Blue*. Other illnesses: congenital heart malformation, etc.
>
> *Grey*. Chorea witnessed in acute attack, not (on first examination) showing evidence of past or present carditis.
>
> *Green*. Cases in which diagnosis was definitely
>
> non-rheumatic
>
> non-choreic.

In these cases I recommended no restriction of activity, and I made an attempt to give an alternative diagnosis. It happened that about 50 percent of the cases had green folders (non-rheumatic)."[93]

The categories put into practice Plato's and Zhuang Zhou's procedure of thinking "according to the joints," of seeking finer distinctions and spacings in reality, which thinking may track without imposing an alien conceptual form of its own invention. Winnicott's analytical "knife" carves an alternative system of classification, which goes against the medical consensus of the time but is attentive to changing circumstances, such as "the disappearance of the rheumatic scourge in London."[94] The jointure of this work—the jointure at which this work works—is multifaceted: in it, not only the body and the mind, but also historical circumstances, environmental influences, epidemiological tendencies, and related situational factors are combined . . . and drawn apart.

It is worth recalling that Winnicott had a long and illustrious career as a pediatrician before venturing into child psychology. His hesitancy to diagnose rheumatic disease immediately upon the presentation of relevant symptoms is, therefore, not part of a psychological or psychologicist prejudice. In fact, since the 1920s, Winnicott specialized in sudden-onset childhood rheumatisms, also focusing on the cardiac complications of these.[95] To object to the use of diagnoses such as "pre-rheumatic" for the roughly 50 percent of the cases gathered in "green" folders was an act of professional defiance and a paradigm change within the profession itself.

His daring gesture should be understood, beyond the field of pediatric medicine, in the context of Winnicott's questioning of another nexus, another joint, namely that of thinking and the unconscious:

> Man the feeler, man the intuitive, far from leaving the unconscious out of account, has always been swayed by his unconscious. But man the thinker has not yet realized that he can both think and also at the same time include the unconscious in his thinking. . . . Do we not see economists

> leaving out of account unconscious greed, politicians ignoring repressed hate, doctors unable to recognize the depression and hypochondria that underlie such illnesses as rheumatism and that impair the industrial machine?[96]

What does it mean to "include the unconscious in . . . thinking," though? On the one hand, the unconscious may be an object of thinking, as it effectively is in psychoanalysis. On the other hand, it may be factored in as a subjective motivation, steering behaviors and symptoms alike behind the subject's back. But there is also a third possibility, where, beyond the limits of subjective and objective conditions, (conscious) thinking and the unconscious form a joint, a continuous and discontinuous, connected and subdivided figure of thought.

• • •

Joints are not to be conflated with folds. Folds are creases in the immanence of the same substance, the folding and unfolding self-divisions of the one. Joints, conversely, unite and separate at least two, animating the infinity that flourishes between them. Mental joints are not psychic folds; they are something other than pleats that temporarily stand out from and are smoothed over into a homogeneous fabric of the mind, and something other, also, than ripples on water. Even when they hold the bones closely together, as in the sutures, what joints throw into relief are the edges, the discontinuities, the non-wholeness of the things they interrelate. Mental joints holding the psyche together and mobilizing its parts are the points where the discrete edges of psychic surfaces meet.

• • •

Discussing the role of joints in the composition of the body, it would be unpardonable to disregard the relation between microcosmic and macrocosmic corporealities, the bodies of biological organisms and of the universe at large. A staple of ancient cosmologies and medieval mysticisms, strict correlations between the two levels of corporeal existence nonetheless look strange to a modern eye.

In Vedic hymns, which are some of the oldest texts in Indian traditions, the body of the world is a hinge or a joint (*saṃdhi*) of heaven and earth, articulated by the god Indra. "The one [*eko*]—Indra—filled the two [*dve*]—earth and heaven—the joint repositories of goods. And from the midspace, at their joint [i.e., of heaven and earth], as charioteer of refreshment (bring) us prizes in yoke together, o champion!" (*RV* III.30.11).[97] It is the midspace of the heavenly-earthly joint, or the horizon, that showers blessings upon all, between the two articulated by the one (god). Separately, the earth and heaven do not yield any goods; the blessings they bestow are concentrated in the relatively thin and delicate livable zone in-between. Their yoking together represents the connection between the body and spirit, which is honed in yogic practice.

(It bears mentioning that *saṃdhi* is also a phonetic joint, a "euphonic combination . . . of two vowels or two consonants or one vowel and one consonant resulting from their close utterance."[98] Here, too, articulation works across both spatial and linguistic connections, between the elements—such as the earth and the sky—and between sounds. The bodies of the world and of language are not only analogous; they share their joints. That is why and how spoken or written languages lend us access to the world.)

The centrality of joints in human bodies is evident particularly in the healing hymns in the *Rigveda*. An exhortation against disease lists all the organs, from which the disease is to be expelled, but the "whole body" is associated, in the last instance, with joints. "I tear out the disease," the hymn proclaims, "from every limb, from every hair, what is born in every joint [*parvani-parvani*]; I tear this disease here out—from your whole body" (*RV* X.163.6).[99] Despite their fragmentary and partial nature, joints comprise the body in its wholeness, just as the joint of heaven and earth establishes the entirety of the livable milieu. Here, too, the in-between is critical. In an idiosyncratic healing hymn addressed to plants, we read: "Him whose every limb, every joint you slither over [*parus paruh*], from him thrust aside the sickness, like a mighty (man) lying in the middle" (X.97.12).[100] Plants thrive in the middle between heaven and earth, which they span, and they act in the middle, in the joints, where their mediational power increases exponentially—"like a mighty (man) lying in the middle"—providing humans with the much-needed healing.

Piecing the universe together at its joints is not an entirely peaceful endeavor. Nor is that of piecing together human corporeity. To assemble the world of the elements, Indra needs to defeat Vr̥tra, a *danava*, or minor deity, blocking the course of cosmic waters. So, "when his battle fury smoked, he [Indra], breaking Vr̥tra apart, joint by joint [*parvaśo rujan*], sent the waters to the sea" (*RV* VIII.6.13).[101] As a result of Indra's actions, waters can start flowing again and reunite with their proper element. Liberation is not a smooth process: a disjoining (of obstacles, obstructions, blockages symbolized by Vr̥tra) must happen before the jointure of the world is accomplished. Nowhere is this co-implication of breaking and putting together the joints as blatant as in hymn VIII.7 to Maruts, the storm deities, who act with Indra and Trita: "They put together the great waters, together the two 'opponents' [heaven and earth], together the sun, together the mace, joint by joint. They drove Vr̥tra apart, joint by joint [*sam vajram parvaśo dadhuh*], apart the mountains lacking rules [radiance], performing a bullish manly deed" (VIII.7.22–23).[102]

The repeated formulation "joint by joint" emphasizes a deep connection between the gathering of the elements and the dispersion of obstacles. The fate of the world rides on actions that are performed on and with joints. (I note, in passing, that Vṛtra's dismantling "joint by joint" indicates a certain inner ordering of the obstacles to cosmic waters, rather than their purely negative, obstructive nature. This contrasts with the hymn's contention that the mountains were "lacking rules [radiance]," the orderly and shining articulation, which the Greek term *kosmos* will also connote.) A combination of the elements "joint by joint" does not obviate the oppositional nature of that which is yoked together in this assemblage, such as "the two 'opponents,'" heaven and earth. Liberated from Vṛtra, "the great waters" do not flow freely but are channeled—both according to elemental justice, rushing toward their own element, the sea, and according to the proportionality required for the livable interval to come into existence. The joints, at which the elements are newly attached to one another, are the sites of finite, occasionally self-undermining, freedom.

The body of a human being is also invigorated and strung together at the joints, in the manner of the body of the world. In a hymn to Soma, the god of the moon, the miraculous properties of the homonym "soma," the drink, are invoked. The life-giving fluid that is soma does wonders to the joints: "These glorious (drops), when drunk, seek wide space. As cows [leather straps] do a chariot, it [soma] knots (me) together in my joints [*gāvah sam anāha parvasu*]" (*RV* VIII.48.5).[103] The joints hold the body together as leather straps hold a chariot, while soma invigorates the joints, upholding what holds the body together. The supportive action of soma implies that joints are insecure points of attachment, in part due to their looseness required for mobility and in part due to their propensity to wear out. Detachment is the underside of attachment, requisite for life and pointing toward death, the dissolution of the body. In other words, strife persists in the corporeal assemblage at the micro-level, just as it remains at the elemental macro-level. The role of soma is to rebind the bond, to reaffirm it without doing away with the unbinding in its midst (when all is said and done, its drops "when drunk, seeks wide spaces," perhaps narrowing these spaces down but not closing them off entirely), to minimize the internal tensions among elements in a finite assemblage—for the time being.

...

Joints are articulated and articulating in three distinct ways: (1) within organs (e.g., hinge joints in arms or legs); (2) between organs (e.g., ball-and-socket joints in shoulders and hips); and (3) between the body and the world. The third articulation is not as evident as the first two, lacking as it does any definite and identifiable anatomical structures. Nevertheless, it is the raison d'être of the other, more concrete articulations. To wrap our heads around this idea, it will be helpful to go back to the main classificatory distinction between mobile and immobile joints. Although these appear to be contraries, they have a common point of reference: positionality. The difference is that, after an early period of flexibility, immobile joints fix the positions of bones they suture together (and even this fixing is not as permanent as we tend to imagine it), while mobile joints enable movement, which is, at bottom, a sequence of positional changes. Since position is a relative category, bodily movements that depend on changes of position result from relational changes, and these correspond to the three articulated-articulating sites of the joints. So, what changes in movement is (1) the position of a part of an organ vis-à-vis another part of the same organ, (2) the position of an organ vis-à-vis another organ or part of the same body, and (3) the position of the entire body vis-à-vis its spatio-material supports and surroundings. With care and patience, the same logic should be applied to psychic joints and to psychosomatic articulations.

...

In a later Vedic tradition, joints are front and center in curative practices, intended to restore a broken, injured, or sickly body. The hymns of the *Atharvaveda* often associate joints with wholeness and health. Harking back to the *Rigveda*'s reference to leather straps that hold a chariot together, the *Atharvaveda*'s charm for curing fractures with *lâkshâ* intones: "Thy marrow shall unite with marrow, and thy joint (unite) with joint. . . . If he has been injured by falling into a pit, or if a stone was cast and hurt him, may he (Dhâtar, the fashioner) fit him together, joint to joint, as the wagoner (Ribhu) [fits together] the parts of a chariot!" (*AV* I.IV.12.3–7).[104] Dhâtar, the creator god, and Ribhu, the divine artisan, are likened to one another and to a resin produced by secretions of the insect *Laccifer lacca*, or shell lac, resulting from the bugs' processing of the sap found in certain plants. Itself a joint between vegetal and animal life activity, *lâkshâ* is raised to the status of a demiurge, "fitting together" living bodies and the entire livable realm. A natural-artificial structure, the joint spans the image of a contraption, such as a chariot, and of a biological body with its secretions. More importantly, it is a part that, by fitting with other parts, allows the whole to be assembled, to be the whole that it is and to function as it should.

Because joints are parts that are crucial for the constitution of the whole, that which threatens the whole—its health and integrity—is thought to reside in them. Quite frequently, the hymns of the *Atharvaveda* locate the hotspot of illness in joints. The charm "to secure perfect health" announces in its concluding portion, which echoes the *Rigveda*'s diagnosis: "The disease that is in thy every limb, thy every hair, thy every joint; that which is seated in thy skin, with Kasyapa's charm, that tears out, to either side we do tear it out" (*AV* I.II.32.7).[105] In a prayer to salve (*âñgana*, a sort of ointment) as a "protector of life and limb," the imploration is this: "From him over whose every limb and every joint thou passest, O salve, thou dost as a mighty interceptor, drive away disease" (II.IV.9.4).[106] If disease resides in the joints, its *locus essendi* is not the depths of amorphous flesh, but the connections that lend to the whole its shape and endow it with mobility. Here, too, disease is understood as a problem of jointure, of the joints in the body and of joints between this body and the embodied spirit, the breath of life, *âtman*.[107]

Continuing to compare the bodily frame with constructed artifacts (such as a chariot), other hymns in the *Atharvaveda* treat the body as a dwelling, a house that, upon death, is handed over to Agni, the god of fire active in funeral pyres. After it was a "receptacle for soma," the body becomes "a house for Agni" (*AV* IX.IX.3.7), who, while momentarily inhabiting it, will not just destroy it in the flames but will shake it loose, so as to rebuild it otherwise.[108] Agni is asked: "Return to him in the other world, firmly bound, ornamented, the house, which we loosen limb by limb, and joint by joint!" (IX.IX.3.10)[109] While the relative disruption of the assemblage that is the body by disease is something to ward off, its absolute disjointure after death is welcomed in the hopes of a future restitution of the body-house "in the other world." Taking this analogy further, disease may be construed as a modified fire, active in the articulations of the body. When the flames of illness complete their work, the energy of the funeral fire will take it further still, dismantling the previous dwelling of life brick by brick, loosening it at the limbs and joints. Agni materially analyzes bodies, discerning their smallest bits in keeping with his designation as Jataveda, "knowing all of existence." But even at this point his work is not yet accomplished. As the hymn proclaims, Agni will restitute to the remains a shining form, "ornamented" and "firmly bound." He will build a new dwelling, focusing on the joints, working with the joints, so that the body is held together once again.

We will have recognized in Agni's activity of disjoining a body the toil of Indra, recounted in the *Rigveda*, the way Indra dismembers Vṛtra (who blocks cosmic waters) "joint by joint"—the same expression as the one used to describe Agni's effect on the "house" that is the body he now indwells. Every sacrificial or funereal rite replays the drama of cosmogony and theomachy, of elemental strife and harmony. The shaking loose of the body at its joints and limbs bespeaks release, liberation, unblocking. It is the release of the body from its previous form. It is, likewise a trace of the liberation of cosmic waters at the demise of Vṛtra. And finally, it is the unblocking of the order of time, that is, of a future that will clamor for the restitution of the past, for the return of each elemental part back to its proper element or of a form to that which has been deformed. The joints are the sites for the articulation of a body, of corporeal existence animated by the breath of life that is the *âtman*, and of climates, elements, worlds (of the living and the dead). A mediator, fire/Agni is a joint between these different regions, much like plants that mediate between the lucidity of the sky and the dense obscurity of the earth.

On Sutures, or the In-Between

Like hinges, sutures are artifacts, but they acquire a biological meaning when they come to refer to a certain kind of joint. Sutures are "the immovable joints peculiar to the vault of the skull."[110] This has not always been the case: "At birth and for several months afterwards, the cranial bones are united by membrane to form the soft spots or fontanelles of the infant skull. These membranous unions gradually disappear as cranial bones grow, make contact, and interlock at their margins. Joints whose bones articulate without intervening soft tissue are known as *synostoses* (Gr., *os* = bone)."[111]

Sutures are peculiar joints, because they seem only to conjoin and to unite, not to disjoin. Their immobility, consequently, disrupts the self-disruption we have come to associate with joints: broken articulations, vulnerable, granting freedom of movement at the expense of stability. That said, sutures smuggle the characteristics of other kinds of joints through the back door, as it were.

First, while synostoses dispense with the interventions of soft tissue, the bones they conjoin do not fuse together. Separation persists as a trace of prior disunity, a barely visible scar engraved on osseous structures and revealing the fake wholeness of the vault that is the cranium. In some cases, these traces or scars can be more visible than in others. For example, the skull of Immanuel Kant had a persistent frontal suture, or metopic suture, bisecting the frontal bone not only in the philosopher's infancy and childhood, but throughout his life. An issue of the *American Journal of Neurology and Psychiatry* from the end of the nineteenth century thus reports, with great puzzlement, that "remarkably enough, the skull of the great German philosopher, Kant, exhibited the frontal suture, which has ordinarily been held to be in itself a sign of low development."[112] The authors of the report, C. Kupffer and F. Bessel, reassure readers that this unusual feature was all but compensated by the extraordinarily large volume of his skull (1,740 cubic centimeters for Kant's overall height of "little over five feet"). Still, as soon as joints appear on stage, everything is complicated and hierarchies crumble: the low becomes high, the fused is disunited, and vice versa.

Second, while separation is secondary in the proper functioning of suture joints, it is primary in the developmental sequence. The immobile joints that are the sutures are initially mobile, and, in fact, remain subtly so for almost the entire life of an individual, until their total ossification in old age.[113] In sutures, the opposites of mobility and immobility are distributed in time, rather than merely in space, as observed in synovial joints. If they preserve a speculative dialectical architecture in the temporal dimension, more so than in space, then sutures may be of great interest as the joints of time (which may occasionally, often, or chronically be *out of joint*).

Sutures are fibrous joints divided into several types, such as serrate, denticulate, or plane, among others.[114] Whatever the type, sutures are all about the mutual fit of edges. Denticulate sutures, for instance, are cognate with the serrated ones, but their interdigitated edges "exhibit a 'dovetail' effect, with the teeth widening toward the ends, which more effectively locks the suture."[115] In woodworking, their analogues are finger joints, also known as comb joints, comprised of interlocking pieces of wood. Thinner or thicker, edges are the places where two or more surfaces meet and, in the case of suture joints (as well as their artisanal counterparts), are intercalated. They are the more or less rugged ends of one surface that are also the beginnings of the other, their undulations, protrusions, and recesses welcoming the mirror opposites that fit them like a glove. In a comparable manner, *suture* sutures together organismic joints and wood joints, nature and culture, elements of woodworking and surgical sewing.

...

The history of anatomy's relation to sutures is as rugged as these joints themselves. It is no longer "an accepted anatomical dogma" that sutures are, in fact, immovable: "Like all joints, the undulating interdigitations of the cranial sutures are designed to facilitate certain motion and to restrict other motion, thus fulfilling the dual function of providing both stability and motility."[116] The cranial vault is not as secure as we thought it was; chunks of its walls change their positions vis-à-vis one another, quickly in childhood and more slowly in adulthood. Certainly, the flexibility of suture joints diminishes with age, but rarely do they become totally fixed. The trajectory of the history of anatomy with regard to sutures is, therefore, the inverse of the sutures' own fate between cranial bones. The understanding of sutures as joints becomes more flexible, putting in doubt the initial conception of immovable articulations, whereas the sutures themselves gradually, if not completely, lose their flexibility in the lifetime of an individual. Infancy and old age, ends and beginnings, swap places in the orders of knowing and existing.

The spatiotemporal serrations of the two orders fit together thanks to the fact that their outlines are back-to-front in relation to each other.

...

Although *suture* is only briefly mentioned on two occasions in Jacques Lacan's 1964 seminar *The Four Fundamental Concepts of Psychoanalysis*, it has far-reaching consequences. Its initial textual appearance is undecidable: it is unclear whether the suture pertains to an arthro-skeletal or a skin-based image of the psyche. Neurosis, Lacan tells those in attendance, brings to light the Kantian gap (*béance*, a gaping hole, a wound) that separates understanding from reality.[117] But it brings this gap to light very late, since neurosis pretends to cure the wound and instead generates another illness in the form of the scar left behind: "Once this gap has been filled, is the neurosis cured? After all, the question remains open. But the neurosis becomes something else, sometimes a mere illness, a *scar* [cicatrice], as Freud said—the scar, not of the neurosis, but of the unconscious."[118]

The subsequent question is about nothing less than the fate of mental scars in psychoanalysis, and it is in Lacan's response to this question that the word "suture" crops up: "The unconscious had closed itself up against his [Freud's] message thanks to those active practitioners of orthopaedics [*ces actifs orthopédeutes*] that the analysts of the second and third generation became, busying themselves, by psychologizing analytic theory, in suturing this gap [*à suturer cette béance*]. Believe me, I myself never re-open it without great care."[119]

Lacan's image of scar tissue evokes a skin-based model of the soul, but the "active practitioners of orthopaedics" who were the second- and third-generation analysts after Freud concerned themselves with the skeletal structure of the psyche. The two models diverge on the shape, place, and meaning (or lack thereof) of gaps and sutures. Whether the gap is that of wounded soft tissue or the in-between space of the joint, however, Lacan rails against its eventual obfuscation. A careful incision made at the site of the scar and attention paid to the place of the joint are necessary for the unconscious issue not to sink deeper into itself and to cease registering as a problem. A certain un-suturing is the sine qua non of Lacanian psychoanalysis.

"Suture" sutures together (and separates: in a word, articulates, creates a jointure between) deep structures and superficial layers, openness and closure, conscious life and the unconscious, well-being and maladjustment. A good suture shows itself, dispensing with the illusion of seamlessness. Being mindful of the gap and of wounded tissue that is still torn and festering under the outer appearance of a scar is more conducive to mental health than the ideal of wholeness. Hegel's line about "the wounds of spirit," *die Wunden des Geistes*,[120] could not be more different from the Lacanian interpretation of the scars of the unconscious, and yet the undecidability of the suture has a Hegelian feel to it. Are sutures there to do away with a gaping wound or with a gap between cranial bones? Are they intended to preserve this wound or this gap? Or . . . do they preserve them by doing away with them? This last formulation approximates the notion of *Aufhebung*, of sublation, at the same time canceling out and maintaining, negating and reaffirming, that which is sublated. Effectively, each joint, including its anatomical structure and action, is *Aufhebung* embodied, a thesis which does not in the least contradict my earlier assertion that the being of spirit is the joint, seeing that the being of spirit is the most comprehensive *Aufhebung*.

When Lacan returns to the suture in response to a query by a participant in the 1964 seminar, he homes in on the moment of non-identity in identification. In a session on "What Is a Picture?" Michel Tort asks about divergent orders of temporality in the act of seeing. Lacan responds: "Look, what I noticed . . . was the suture [*j'ai marqué . . . la suture*], the pseudo-identification, that exists between what I called the time of terminal arrest of the gesture and what, in another dialectic that I called the dialectic of identificatory haste, I put as the first time, namely, the moment of seeing. The two overlap, but they are certainly not identical, since one is initial and the other terminal."[121] He will then add: "The moment of seeing can intervene here only as a suture [*ne peut intervenir ici que comme suture*], a conjunction [*jonction*] of the imaginary and the symbolic, and it is taken up again in a dialectic, that sort of temporal progress that is called haste, thrust, forward movement, which is concluded in the *fascinum*."[122]

Without going into the details of the dialectic, we discern in it the three main domains of Lacanian psychoanalysis: the imaginary and the symbolic, in addition to the real, which begins, for us, with the gap between understanding and reality, with a hole or a wound. The suture as a "pseudo-identification" is the surgical sewing up of and the hastening of scar-formation ("that sort of temporal progress that is called haste") over the wound. In this sense, the suture is the double-stitched seam of the imaginary and the symbolic, overlapping but "not identical" to one another and overlaying the gap of the real—which can only be approached as such solely from the side of the suture. Very quickly, though, the sense of the suture changes; Lacan transforms it from the surgical means for wound closure to a joint, a junction or a conjunction (*jonction*) of the imaginary and the symbolic that are interrelated through the (still unnamed) void of the real. So determined, the site of the suture is the skull—the outer casing of the brain indirectly influencing and influenced by the inner, as Hegel has it—and the moment of seeing is also possible thanks to holes in the skull, the eye sockets, or the upper caves of the body, for Irigaray, who, at least on this page of my book, gets the last word.

...

Thanks to sutures, things somehow hold together without being whole. This is true for joints and stitches that, in combining what is torn or discontinuous, reveal discontinuity *as* discontinuity. Linking shards or pieces of flesh, skin or bones, sutures mend fragmentation without the pretense of totalization, without the illusion of original wholeness. If the whole has never actually existed, then mending-suturing is the alpha and omega of being; world repair is the making of a world (of a psyche, of life).

...

Alain Badiou shares with Lacan an obsession with removing sutures, picking at them and on them. In *Manifesto for Philosophy*, sutures are said to betray philosophy in its free play between four conditions: the poetic, the mathematical, the political, and the amorous. Betrayal consists in a practice whereby "philosophy *delegates* its functions to one or other of its conditions." "I shall call this type of situation a *suture*," Badiou announces. "Philosophy is placed in suspension every time it presents itself as being sutured to one of its conditions."[123] Furthermore, the main suture, by virtue of which philosophy has been suspended at least since the nineteenth century, is science: "The suture of philosophy to its scientific condition progressively reduces it to be but mere analytic quibbling, whose language *bears the brunt* in every sense of the term."[124] *A* condition thus becomes *the* condition—indeed, the precondition—of philosophy, which dissolves into it without remainder.

Aside from an obsession with un-suturing, Badiou also shares with Lacan a rather limited vision of the suture. The limitation is quantitative, modal, and unipolar (positive).

Quantity. There is rarely only one suture; in isolation, its act of holding together the disparate fails. In wounds, let alone between the bones of the skull, sutures are always in the plural. Likewise in the title of Badiou's own text, the sixth chapter of his *Manifesto*. Nonetheless, the purported fault of the suture (in the singular) is its exclusivity: it names the situation, in which philosophy abrogates all of its allegiances but one.

Modality. After the quantitative reduction of suture*s* to suture, Badiou skips over its indeterminacy (if not its overdetermination). For him, suturing is determining the event of philosophy in terms, for example, of a scientific endeavor and, as a result, giving up on this event's fourfold configuration. Yet, sutures are indeterminate with regard to their belonging to skin or bones, emerging in surgical interventions or in organismic development. Their semantic and other possibilities are a good match for the "free play" of possibilities defining philosophy itself.

Unipolarity. Badiou assumes that the function of the suture is to eliminate difference, to fuse, to diffuse, to dissolve philosophy by equating it to one of its conditions. But, be they stitches or joints, the place of sutures is in-between, valorizing neither the negative nor the positive moment of the relation they establish. Every suture is as much a suturing together as an un-suturing; every suture undoes itself all by itself. To insist on un-suturing is still to rotate in the semantic orbit of the suture.

What Badiou decries as the reduction and loss of philosophy sutured to one of its conditions is the signature operation of metaphysics. Reluctant as Badiou is to use Heidegger's conceptual apparatus and eager as he might be to define philosophy "other than from its history, other than from the destiny and decline of Western metaphysics,"[125] he provides fodder aplenty for the interpretation of suturing as a metaphysical gesture. To resort to his own terms, metaphysics is a meta-suturing, insistent on the oneness, rigid determination, and the polarity of sameness at the expense of multiplicity, possibility, and difference. This means that metaphysics constantly struggles against and tries to suppress an inner instability, and that deconstruction does nothing more (and nothing less) than retrieve and reinforce this preexisting instability.

As he examines the suturing of philosophy to its various conditions, Badiou confesses that the suture is not one. "But in the final analysis, as in the 'materialist' vision, science is sent back to its technico-historic conditions, the double suture is articulated under the dominance of the political, which alone can *also* totalize science, as we saw when the same Stalin meddled with the legislation of genetics, linguistics or relativistic physics, in the name of the proletariat and its own Party."[126] What is gleaned "in the final analysis" changes Badiou's preliminary definition of the suture. It turns out that, to be sutured, philosophy cannot delegate its functions to just one of its four conditions. In funneling philosophy's energy of free play to a restrictive determination, there is always "*also*" (note the italicization of this word in the text) "the dominance of the political." The apparently single and singular suture is invariable double, arousing the suspicion that the other two limitations imputed to it (namely, the modal and the unipolar) also do not stand. Accomplishing the reverse of what Badiou ascribes to it, the indeterminacy of the suture breaks through in this multiplication of conditional restrictions, where continuity is of a piece with disruption and where *only* is not incompatible with *also*.

Badiou's solution to the impasse of a philosophy lost in its restrictive suturing is the system. "Philosophy is only de-sutured," he writes, "if it is, on its own, systematic. If *a contrario* philosophy declares the impossibility of the system, it is because it is sutured, and hands thought over to only one of its conditions."[127] Let's ignore the inexplicable reversion to "only one of its conditions," when "in the final analysis" the suture is ineluctably double (X + political). The reason for Badiou's failure to register the indeterminacy of the suture is the same as the reason for his conviction that "the possibility of the system" clashes with the non- or anti-system. As a joint, the suture is part of a non-system of articulations that make the skeleto-muscular system what it is. "Compossibility,"[128] a word Badiou stresses as he describes the state of philosophy in the free play of its fourfold, is the joint possibility *and* impossibility of the system, its dependence on elements that are not and can never be systematized. The arthrological sense of suture should have given Badiou pause.

...

Rather than and before "the symbolic," the symbol itself is a suture. In ancient Greece, a *sumbolon* (literally, "thrown together," *sum* + *ballein*) was comprised of two parts of a broken coin, bone, piece of wood, or another object. Parties to a contract, relatives, or lovers who would endure years of separation, or a future recipient of a message and a messenger, would be given one part of the *sumbolon* each. At their eventual meeting, the halves would be brought together, validating the authenticity of a relation, a message, or a legal document. A symbol, then, is never entirely whole. It is only momentarily sutured on the special occasion of an encounter, and its suturing requires brokenness. Being drawn apart in space is the precondition for its articulation. No matter how physically far from one another the two parts of a *sumbolon* are, they are thrown together. Their temporal trajectories are contemporaneous.

...

The non-systemic place of a suture in the system is elucidated in Jacques-Alain Miller's study of this Lacanian term. In his contribution to the inaugural issue of *Cahiers pour l'analyse*, Miller sets out the program of his text as follows: "*Cet exposé est pour articuler le concept de la suture, non dit comme tel par Jacques Lacan, bien qu'à tout instant présent dans son système* [It is the objective of this paper to articulate the concept of suture which, if it is not named as such by Jacques Lacan, is constantly present in his system]."[129] Not by accident, the constant presence of the suture is unnamed as such. In a reading of Frege, Miller points out the act of excluding "*la fonction du sujet, en tant qu'elle supporte les opérations de l'abstraction et de unification* [the function of the subject, as support of the operations of abstraction and unification]."[130] The "function of the subject" is the suture itself, that is, suture is "*le rapport du sujet à la chaîne de son discours* [the relation of the subject to the chain of its discourse]," which, more broadly, is "*le rapport en général du manque à la structure dont il est élément, en tant qu'il implique position d'un tenant-lieu* [the relation in general of lack to the structure, in which it is an element, insofar as it implies the position of taking place]."[131]

The suture as lack within the structure in which it figures and which it constitutes is not perceived as such within the confines of that structure. To diagnose the lacuna that it is, one needs to take a step back: it is outside the structure (of discourse, or of any other body) that the suture or the function of the subject becomes visible—as an absence. From within, one experiences illusory wholeness, the lack of the lack that is the suture, precisely due to the effects of the unnoticed suture itself, be it a stitch or a joint. But from without, when the suture appears as what it is, all of a sudden it is presented as the opposite of what it conveys: a gap, instead of a tight connection.

The suture's counteraction, acting in the first instance against itself, is to be expected. A joint is a broken articulation; a stitch mends a tear in the skin before dissolving and being replaced with a scar. This is the logic of relations, more so than of signifiers, mentioned in the subtitle of Miller's work. The suture's sustained disappearance, its self-undermining, ensures the appearance of terms in a relation, in a system, in a chain of discourse. But that is not all. When the suture is erased, the non-identity of the thing, which never coincides with itself, is supplanted by the identity of the object, as the one: "*Par où vous voyez la disparition qui doit s'effectuer de la chose pour qu'elle apparaisse comme objet—qui est* la chose en tant qu'elle est une [Whence you can see the disappearance of the thing which must be in effect in order for it to appear as object—which is *the thing insofar as it is one*]."[132] The suture is the function of the subject, giving itself an object as a replacement for the thing, which is, to invert Miller's terms, an object that is not one. The suture, then, is an articulation of the subject-object relation, exceptional among relations.

That said, the subject-object relation is lopsided. The suture as the function of the subject does not allow it to appear in the world as any other object would. The subject is never one; it resembles more a thing than an object. That is why it must be attributed the value of zero, rather than one: "*C'est l'énoncé décisif que le concept de la non-identité-à-soi est assigné par le nombre zéro qui suture le discours logique* [It is this decisive proposition that the concept of non-identity-to-self is assigned the number zero, which sutures logical discourse]."[133] The non-identity of the suture looms large over its meanings, from joints to stitches. It is the same indeterminacy and metonymic instability as that of the Greek *arthron*, the articulation, the joint, which may refer to any organ whatsoever. Does this mean that in the universe of objects, too, there are those (like sutures, like joints) that in their non-self-identity are closer to subjects and things than to the rest of objects? Are they exceptions to or more acute expressions of the general rule, according to which the oneness of every object is impermanent and, while it lasts, extremely costly energy-wise, necessitating regular maintenance and upkeep? Is every one within the system not only already-not- and not-yet-zero, but also, beneath the trappings of its self-identity, always-already-zero?

...

The mobility of cranial sutures, contrasted with the stability of cranial bones, is an apt image of the subject, as opposed to an object. The findings of histological studies indicate that "there may be partial sutural fusion, but only at a relatively old age. Cranial sutures in the pig-tailed macaque are not fused by the 20th year and in humans by the 90th year."[134] If sutures do not allow the skull to close, to coincide with itself, then even the material "casing" of the brain participates in the essential instability of the subject and should be assigned "the number zero, which sutures logical discourse." The skull itself tells us: "Suture is openness."

...

A certain confusion ensues in the subject-object distinction. Any objective element is at least potentially subjective, to the extent that the object's repression of the thing's non-identity is never totally successful, that is, to the extent that openness persists in a sutured closure, tight as it might be. Animism is the pinnacle of this tendency, encouraging the eruption of the thing that is not one from beneath the death mask of the object's identity. So, the function of the subject may be exercised by *anything*: by *any thing that remains a thing, rather than an object*.

Given the distension of the function of the subject, Slavoj Žižek's reflections on the suture require a careful rereading. Žižek writes: "The element which holds together the two levels [essence and appearances], 'suturing' each of them, functions as their quilting point, and the repetition (of the *Möbius* strip) . . . takes the form of an inversion in the way sutures function: the 'inside' (the space of the signifier) has to be sutured by an additional element which holds within the signifying order the place of what is excluded from it . . . , and external reality itself has to be sutured by an element which holds in it the place of the symbolic process (*objet a*)."[135] He adds: "The notion of the suture, 'materialist' as it may appear to be, has to be supplemented by its inversion: the 'external reality,' in order to attain full existence, has to be supplemented ('sutured') by a 'subjective' element."[136]

Although the subjective element seems superfluous within the order of pure objectivity, this very order ("external reality") cannot come into being without the subjective suture. The supplement of the apparently materialist side of the suture, where exteriority is symptomally expressed within "the closed circle of representation,"[137] reads like a textbook case of idealism, in which the subject underwrites the existence of reality. Žižek's point, however, is that the side purporting to be purely materialist in opposition to the idealist supplement acts out something like a distorted version of idealism. Alternatively, the materialism of the suture, which accommodates the extremes of classical materialism and idealism, is an effect of articulation, of the jointure that it is. The Möbius strip is the smooth, undisrupted (less dialectical, as well) figure of the inversions typical of a joint.

One way to get a hang of the dizzying transitions Žižek signals is by tracking the relative terms "inside" and "outside." External reality is external *not* to the subject, but to the function of the subject, which at the same time confronts it in the shape of the signifying order and underlies it as the irrepressible force of the thing overflowing the identity of an object. The "external" is itself a suture, keeping apart and conjoining, resisting and outlining, two functions of the subject. The materiality of this suture is concentrated in the thickness of its edges—the outer and the inner edges of the external. The interiority of the external is the objective and objectifying mask of the thing; the exteriority of the external is the very interiority of the signifying order. The inversions of the suture occur on this double edge.

More so than Lacan, Miller, or Badiou, Žižek is attentive to the detotalizing openness of the suture. In an essay specifically dealing with this concept, he writes: "We can see how, in this precise sense, suture is the exact opposite of the illusory self-centred totality that successfully erases the decentred traces of its production process. . . . Suture means that, precisely, such self-enclosure is apriori impossible, that the excluded externality always leaves traces within."[138] At the very least, the suture is ambiguous—a word which Žižek mentions in the title of a section of his essay. It is a trace of the excluded exteriority within, the openness *of* closure, the irreparable fissuring of the absolute.

Joints and Time

In the closing of act 1, scene 5, Shakespeare's Hamlet utters the famous lines: "The time is out of joint. O cursed spite / That ever I was born to set it right!" (*Hamlet*, 1.5.943–44). Time's being out of joint is the apparition of his dead father's ghost, the eruption of the past in the present, an absence that is both absent and present. And it is also the injustice of regicide, the murder of the father by Hamlet's uncle, Claudius, who usurps the throne. If "murder [is] most foul, as in the best it is," then "this [one is] most foul, strange, and unnatural" (1.5.763–64). Taking life away from its victim, murder disjoins the order of time, as well as, in Hamlet's case, family ties (between brothers or an uncle and his nephew) and the plan of monarchic succession.

If time can be "out of joint," then the obvious question, rarely if ever raised by commentators, is: What are the joints of time? How can time be *not* out of joint? How can it be properly jointed? Hamlet, after all, laments this particular time, *the* time he is living through, while implicitly suggesting that neither other times nor time as such suffer from the disruption of their articulations. Consequently, justice is the work done on the joints—on time's joints, to be precise—that adjusts their fragile connections, putting them in their rightful places. Time-work as joint-work is the sublime chiropractic exercise of justice.

Still, to get to the bottom of this matter, it is necessary to ask about the joints of time. What are they? To put it bluntly and in a somewhat dry manner, they are the units or the measures of time. Dong Zhongshu, a Chinese philosopher from the Han dynasty (second century B.C.E.) develops the notion of 天人感應 (*tian ren gan-ying*) or the resonance between heavens and human beings, by, among other things, correlating "the human body's 360 joints . . . to the number of days in a year."[139] In the *Chunqui Fanlu* (*Luxuriant Gems of Spring and Autumn*) masterpiece, Dong Zhongshu observes: "The [term] 'body' resembles [the term] 'Heaven.' The numerology of the body and that of Heaven are mutually interwoven. Therefore [the body's] destiny and that of Heaven are mutually linked. Heaven completes the human body with the number of days in a full year. Thus the body's 360 lesser joints correspond to the number of days in a year, and the twelve larger joints match the number of months."[140]

Whether the units of time are bigger or smaller—whether they are days or months—all of them are grafted onto joints. The resemblance of the micro- and the macrocosms is not just spatial, shape-based, positional, or geometrical, but also functional, numeric, and temporal, especially when it comes to the interlinked "destinies" of the body and heaven. In fact, numbers are emphasized in the only other mention of time-joints in the *Chunqui Fanlu*: "Human beings have 360 joints that match Heaven's numbers."[141] Rather than linear sequences, the units of time as joints and as "Heaven's numbers" hold the body together, while affording it motion; they assemble the bodies of heaven and of human beings in coherent, mutually reflecting entities.

The thesis that joints are the units of time, be they months, days, or even instants, may help elucidate the nature of time. It would be a mistake to view them as self-contained, discrete units, because joints are intermediate assemblages, passages in-between, highlighting the crucial activity of time: passing. As embodied transitions, they trouble distinctions between one and two, or one and many; analogously, milliseconds are transitions between seconds, embedded in transitions between minutes, embedded in transitions between hours, embedded in transitions between days, and so on. Time is always in-between, the time of joints—continuous *and* discontinuous. Being out of joint would then mean doing away with the in-between at the extremes of absolute fusion *and* separation. Not least, of time.

...

Time is out of joint. Which joint? Sundry shapes and kinds of joints suggest that time and its "units" are not homogeneous. Some of the time-joints enable movement and, therefore, require a more pronounced discontinuity between the moments they conjoin; others offer more stability, exchanging synovial cavities for symphysis. Time's being out of joint must, likewise, be differentiated. When time is out of the ball-and-socket joint, the epoch is that of dislocation, mimicking a dislocated shoulder. When it is out of the hinge joint, we enter the era of misalignment, aggravating the instability that is inevitable in a synovial type of joint. When time is out of suture joints, it is the epoch of fragmentation. By the looks of it, *our* time is out of joints: fragmented, misaligned, dislocated, running out of the finite infinity of that which lies in-between.

...

The scheme of time-as-joints is discernible in Aristotle's *Physics*. Time, Aristotle says at the outset of its treatment, is *amudros*, "obscure" (*Phys.* 217b35).[142] That's because an inquiry into its being finds out that time is more intimately related to nonbeing, to nonexistence. Time is a jointure of the no-longer and the not-yet; it con-sists of parts that do not ex-ist (218a2). More than that, the now (*nûn*), which in its presence appears to merge with being itself and is the *is*, internally falls apart into what "is always one and the same" and what "is perpetually different [*heteron*]" (218a11).[143] The now is the joint, because it is itself and not-itself, same and other, capable of accommodating the no-longer and the not-yet within the cavities of its own non-identity.

Aristotle sketches out the formal structure of the joint from the very first lines dedicated to the concept of time in the *Physics*. The functional determinations of joints will crop up soon thereafter. Among the most obvious activities of time, he singles out its acts of moving (*kinêsis*) in passing and changing (*metabolê*, which is a form of movement for Aristotle), and he proposes to focus on the clues provided by moving and changing things (*to kinoumenon kai metaballon*) (*Phys.* 218b10–15).[144] Since articulated animals with muscular-skeletal systems move thanks to their mobile, synovial joints, an implicit clue to the workings of time (at least as experienced from the standpoint of vertebrates) lies in their anatomy. As in these joints, a gap separates one now from another, not to mention the no-longer and the not-yet. This gap or this difference is detectable in an *après coup*, the "afterwards," which makes time what it is (or what it was): "There appears to be no time between two 'nows' when we fail to distinguish them" (218b25–30). Time is "between-time," *to metaxu chronos*—meantime, meanwhile, interval—which is indispensable there where two nows are attached to one another: *sunaptousi gar to proteron nûn tô husteron nûn* (218b25–26).[145] Needless to say, the verb *sunaptein*, to which Aristotle resorts in this passage, means "to conjoin," "to fasten with," and it refers to another word for joint, *hapsos*. This is the closest we get to a definition of the joints of time, or of time as a joint, in his text.

The difference between the previous now and the subsequent now marks the passage (movement) of time. The two nows themselves are articulated around nothing. The psychic dimension of this nothing becomes apparent in not noticing that something has changed, in a lapse of conscious vigilance: "Whenever we recognize that there has been a lapse of time, we by that act recognize that something has been going on" (*Phys.* 219a5–10).[146] We notice *that* we have not noticed change, without (at least without as of yet) noticing *what* had changed and *how*. This is the ever belated "origin" of time. Since time counts, by means of which time is registered and so comes into being, depend on psychic life, this dimension is fundamental, even if it retreats from theoretical view when counting becomes the prerogative of indifferent machines, including watches. (Is there something like time, which depends on the lapse of not-having-noticed, for AI?)

The material dimension of the nothing, around which two distinct nows are articulated, has to do with this middle part being not another now but a sheer difference between the before and the after, between two nows that, despite their identity as being each *now*, are not identical to each other (nor, at bottom, to themselves). This difference is the in-between that, like a mobile joint, renders time itself mobile, puts it in relation to movement without reducing it to movement. Plus, the two elements articulated by nothing are themselves nothing—already or still nothing, a now that has passed and a now that has not yet happened. Time-as-a-joint is an articulation of nothing with nothing by nothing.

...

To see a body from the perspective of the joints: to see time from the interval of nothing. Time is neither an empty continuum a posteriori populated with events nor the a priori fullness of being. It passes—it is in transit, through nothing, from and to nothing. Activating its countless joints, it moves, but the movement seen from the in-between is indistinguishable from rest. In Plato's *Timaeus*, time is said to be the moving image of eternity, *kinêton tina aiônos* (*Tim.* 37d). Nowhere else but at its joints is this eccentric identity of time and eternity, of movement and rest, so glaring.

...

If time has joints, if it is *in* the joints, then it is not nothing. More than that, a body and its organs are the prototypical something. So, how can they house nothing?

In one of the earliest Upanishads (the *Brhadâranyaka Upanishad*, dating back to between the ninth and the sixth centuries B.C.E.), death decides to give itself a body (*âtman*): "In the beginning, there was nothing here at all. Death alone covered this completely, as did hunger; for what is hunger but death? Then death made up his mind: 'Let me equip myself with a body [*âtman*]'" (*BU* 1.2.1).[147] Divided into various domains, the body of death, which is also that of the world, becomes all that is, but in the end, it, too, dies, leaving behind a bloated corpse, still inhabited by a mind. "Then he [death in the shape of the corpse of Aditi] had this desire: 'I wish that this corpse of mine would become fit to be sacrificed so I could get myself a living body [*âtman*]. Then that corpse became a horse" (1.2.7).[148] The second section of the first *adhyaya* (chapter or division) in the *Brhadâranyaka Upanishad*, from which these lines are drawn, narrates the prehistory of the first section, where the partitioning of the body of the horse generates the world. In the order of narration, chronological time is thus disrupted; it is disjointed, and for essential reasons.

The cosmic horse is, to be sure, a sacrificial animal. Its distribution among the diverse regions of existence will give rise to the earth, the sky, and the intermediate region, to celestial bodies, to plant, animal, and human life, to hills, and rivers, and speech. For instance: "The head of the sacrificial horse, clearly, is the dawn—its sight is the sun; its breath is the wind; and its gaping mouth is the fire common to all men. The body of the sacrificial horse is the year" (*BU* I.I.I).[149]

Just as our task is to observe the body from the vantage point of the joints, so the *Brhadâranyaka Upanishad* suggests taking a glance at life from the perspective of death—of a series of deaths, running the gamut from the disembodied primordial death, through death endowed with the body of Aditi and the corpse of death's body, to the corpse's afterlife as a horse and its cosmogenic sacrifice. The horse's joints, in their turn, bear a direct relation to time: "Its limbs are the seasons; its joints are the months and fortnights" (*BU* I.I.I).[150] For limbs to move, they must be articulated by joints; for the rotations of seasons to happen, they must be connected and separated by months, which are the joints imparting mobility to the limbs of time. Unlike most of the correspondences between parts of the sacrificial horse and the universe, though, the joints are said to consist not of one thing only, but of "months and fortnights," that is, of a certain measure of time and of half that measure. The hint is that the interval is indeterminate, infinitely divisible in being slotted between and within seasons. Thus, the year, comprising the entire ensouled body (*âtman*) of the cosmic horse, is an active body capable of moving its limbs, the seasons, which are themselves dependent on the mobility of time's joints.

Contemporaneous with the sacrificial cosmology of the Upanishads, the *Shatapatha Brahmana* (dating back to the sixth or seventh centuries B.C.E.) depicts the world as a "[brick]-built fire-altar [*Agniksetra*]" (X.5.4.I).[151] Here "the function of the heaven and earth [the horizon] is its [circle of] enclosing-stones, for it is beyond the air that heaven and earth meet, and that [junction, *sandhi*] is the [circle of] encircling-stones" (x.5.4.2).[152] The horizon is an articulation of heaven and earth that gives a circular shape to the fire-altar that is the world. By enclosing, it contains but also welcomes the fire in its midst, in the expanse that forms thanks to the heavenly-earthly joint. It is, then, an enclosure that is inherently open, a broken articulation, breathable, windswept, and, as such, letting the fire-altar be what it is. Furthermore, strikingly manifest on the horizon, dawn and dusk are the junctures of light and darkness, the joints of day and night that also bear the name *sandhi*. They are the temporal analogues for the spatial enclosure, variously illuminated or dimmed depending on the cosmic rhythms of celestial fire.

I dare interject here a brief observation regarding the rounding off and the straightness of the appropriate jointures in Indian thought. The horizon, as Agni's altar delimiting the world, is encircling. The relation between the sky and the earth it institutes is curved. The sense of justice inherent in right, in the rightness and uprightness of conduct and being as such, is the opposite: *rta*. At the root of our right, but also rite (in the sense of ritual), *rta* is defined by Charles Malamoud as "the most exact conjoining of all the parts of the universe [*l'exacte articulation de toutes les parties de l'univers*]."[153] Incidentally, it is also the root that is formative of the Greek *arthron*, "joint." Two mutually contradictory images of cosmic joints thus begin to form: the straight and the curved, each of them entailing a different spatio-spiritual sense of being and justice. The place of all ritual sacrifices, the world stage, is itself a circular arena, on which, as which, right actions take place, aided by the minutely adjusted degrees of perfecting heat that cooks the entire world.

According to the earlier stratum of the Vedic tradition of ancient India, "the human body was invested with unparalleled cosmological significance, and parts of the body were homologized with cosmic phenomena."[154] In particular, the creation of the universe ensued from the sacrificial dismemberment of *purusha*, the primeval man. The anthropocentric outlook, which resonates with Dong Zhongshu's *Luxuriant Gems of Spring and Autumn* and with the Judaic/kabbalistic notion of *ha-adam ha-qadmon* or Cosmic Adam, simultaneously invests with a high honor and places a tremendous burden on the human. The world (and time—which, in an important sense, *is* the world) is made out of the primeval man, who stands in a special position vis-à-vis the rest of material existence, not as a blueprint to be transferred from a creative idea to actuality, but as flesh torn to pieces and distributed among disparate parts of the universe that become what they are by means of this partitioning and apportionment.

The Upanishadic text slips a horse in place of the human, who is both dethroned and relieved of the pain of materially subtending, embodying, or enfleshing all existence. Still, with remarkable consistency, joints are associated with time: with days, months, and other such measures. They activate the movements of the world's body, the lines of separation and connections traversing it, and—assuming that the body should be carved at the joints—the principle of distribution, just and minutely adjusted, of the body's parts to the respective elemental ranges they inaugurate. Dwelling in joints, as these very joints of the world, time is more than time: it is justice consistent with finitude, through which nothing—the nothing, the enfleshment of death in mortal creatures—glimmers, faintly and obscurely, appropriate to each being it delimits according to its own self-delimitation as *this* finite being.

...

Synovial joints include a cavity, filled with synovial fluid, which allows the articulated limbs and other parts of the body to move. Apparently, they require a spatial gap in order to do their work. But if movement is indissociable from time, then the gap is also a temporal one. When Aristotle writes that "time is neither identical with movement nor capable of being separated from it" (*Phys.* 219a1–5),[155] he is not merely describing—he is performing the work of time, which is the work of the joints, of continuity and discontinuity, of detachment in attachment and discreteness in flux, of fullness and emptiness. To paraphrase Aristotle, time's joints are neither identical with nothing nor capable of being separated from it.

...

Becoming is the articulation of being and nothing. That is what Hegel conveys in his *Science of Logic* and *Philosophy of Nature*. That is, perhaps, the only thing he conveys, in myriads of variations, in his writings. The first synthesis in the "doctrine of being" in Hegel's *Logic* is that of being and nothing, which yields becoming: "The truth is neither being nor nothing, but rather that being passes over into nothing and nothing into being. . . . Their truth is therefore this *movement* of the immediate vanishing of the one into the other: the *becoming*, a movement in which the two are distinguished, but by a distinction which has just as immediately dissolved itself [das Werden*; eine Bewegung, worin beide unterschieden sind, aber durch einen Unterschied, der sich ebenso unmittelbar aufgelöst hat*]."[156] In *Philosophy of Nature*, Hegel hones the sense of becoming as time: "Time itself is the *becoming*, this coming-to-be and passing away, the *actually existent abstraction*."[157]

We have examined the joints of time thus far. Time itself—Hegel tells us—understood as "the becoming," is a joint between being and nothing. (The nothing of ancient Indian thought reappears in its mediation with being, which permits it to be enfleshed in all that becomes. There is, for all that, no primacy afforded to nothing in Hegel's dialectics of time.) Everything that happens takes place in the double articulation of time, whereby "being passes over into nothing and nothing into being." Provided that this two-way movement of events is *time as a joint*, rather than a *joint of time*, a question arises: In which corporeality is time a joint? Whose body does it mobilize?

In Hegel's philosophical project, time is a joint of spirit, which moves across the articulations of being and nothing, in a becoming that causes the distinction between these extremes to be "dissolved," *aufgelöst.* The dissolution is not tantamount to a sheer disappearance, however. Whereas the wounds of spirit heal without leaving scars behind, the articulations of being and nothing in becoming at the crossing between "coming-to-be and passing away" *are* finite beings. The articulations are, simultaneously, distinctions in the already recognizable dynamics of joints (each thing in the singularity of its identity as what all the other things are *not*), to which Hegel adds the conjunction of the distinct and the indistinct in and as the movement of becoming. The truth (*Wahrheit*) is to be sought in these articulations, without which the being of spirit is *immediately* nothing. The joints of spirit—or, in a word, time—are the mediations of being and nothing, the deferral of an immediate identity of these extremes. Only in this deferral is there something (essentially finite—a being-nothing and a nothing-being). Joints put spirit to work, lending it actuality, if only in the abstract mode of time as an "*actually existent abstraction*," according to Hegel's precise formulation.

After Hegel defines time as "negativity posited for itself [*an sich selbst negative*],"[158] he revisits the issue of actuality, or energy,[159] articulated in time's articulation of being and nothing. "It is because things are finite that they are in time," he writes. "It is not because they are in time that they perish; on the contrary, things themselves are the temporal, and to be so is their objective determination. It is therefore the process of actual things themselves which makes time; and though time is called omnipotent, it is also completely impotent."[160]

The actuality of finite things is the non-transcendental "process . . . which makes time"; it is the energy of the things themselves that articulates being and nothing, the energy or the actuality (*Wirklichkeit*) which, by the same token, forms the body of spirit, capable of moving at its time-joints. Mutatis mutandis, one can predicate of spirit what Hegel predicates of time, notably that it is not because things are in spirit that they are preserved. On the contrary, the things themselves are the actuality of spirit, and to be so is their objective determination. Although spirit is hailed as omnipotent, it is completely impotent. Articulations of time and spirit thread in and out of actuality, inventing fresh and reiterating existent transitions from being to nothing and from nothing back to being.[161]

On Neck and Wrists.

The Pivot Joints, or Turns and Turnings

Pivot joints are, like hinge joints, synovial. Classified as trochoids (from the Greek *trochos*, "wheel"), they are tasked with providing rotation "in only a single plane."[162] One of the most important pivot joints is the atlantoaxial joint at the craniovertebral junction, connecting the C1 and C2 vertebrae in the uppermost part of the spine and the base of the skull, which allows us to turn our heads from side to side. Like hinge joints, it has only one degree of freedom. The distal radioulnar joint is also a pivot, enabling the turning of the wrist, a movement we engage in when unscrewing a lid of a jar or driving a screw into its spot.

Our collective intellectual body has been going through a number of turns recently, putting to work its pivot joints, especially those close to the head. Whether consciously or not, all of them mimic the Heideggerian turn, *die Kehre*. The linguistic turn and the post-human turn, the animal turn and the plant turn, the cultural turn and the material turn, the digital turn and the translational turn, the care turn and the affective turn—already this small sample is sufficient to make one's head spin.

Heidegger at least was adamant that the turn in thinking, which *Being and Time* was meant to embody, had failed, so much so that he charged his subsequent works with the task of providing the rearticulation of the non-articulated (and, to some extent, inarticulable) missing divisions of his magnum opus. Twenty years after its publication and barely two years after the end of the Second World War, he observed that

> the adequate execution and completion of this other thinking that abandons subjectivity is surely made more difficult by the fact that in the publication of *Being and Time* the third division of the first part, 'Time and Being,' was held back. . . . Here everything is reversed. The division in question was held back because everything failed in the adequate saying of this turning and did not succeed with the help of the language of metaphysics. . . . This turning is not a change of standpoint from *Being and Time*, but in it the thinking that was sought first arrives at the location of that dimension out of which *Being and Time* is experienced, that is to say, experienced from the fundamental experience of the oblivion of Being.[163]

What Heidegger tries to convey is that not only his unique *Kehre* but also every turn is a figure of failure, striving but unable to face that which one has to face—in the case of Heidegger, because this is no longer a matter of facing, of an oppositional deadlock of the subject and the object, nor of any vestiges of the subject in thinking.[164] The best we can do is elaborate failure a little better (Beckett's phrase, which has by now become a cliché, immediately comes to mind in this regard), to articulate *it*, this failure, rather than the stated goal itself. A self-conscious turn is conscious, at bottom, of its fundamental failure.

Alas, none of the above considerations are in the air today. One has an impression that turns and turnings are rapidly multiplying, the past supplanted by the present without a chance to grow old. In this day and age, relentless "innovation" is the name of the game: intuit the bend in the road ahead before everyone else does, magnify its significance, and seduce colleagues to flock with you there. Then, with little time to spare, expect another set of turns, leading away from the previous ones and burying them under a pile of clichés, superficial criticisms, and self-serving judgments on how your predecessors did not live up to their promise.

(I will take this occasion to testify, with a hand on my textual heart, to the fact that I have never treated vegetal philosophy in the context of other turns in the humanities. "The Plant Turn" is, for me, a puzzling designation. Vegetal life is not something we have the luxury to turn away from, nor to turn toward, since it surrounds and indwells us, psychically and physically. Instead, it can be subject to repression—a term I prefer to the neutral-sounding "plant blindness"—as it has been throughout much of Western history, *or* it can steer thinking and living along tracks at once infinite and finite, provided that one hears its silent call. At any rate, the phrase "plant turns" appeals to me much more than "the Plant Turn," not least because plants practice many kinds of turning, from circumnutation to metamorphoses or becoming-as-turning, which have incomparably more degrees of freedom than the pivot joints of our collective intellectual body would accommodate.)

Despite a slew of turns, nothing changes substantially. These turns are not revolutions, but revolts, taking place on the same plane, rotating around a single axis. Their truth, moreover, lies in what they are turning away from, namely the human or the anthropocentric, the idealist or the metaphysical, planes of thought and imagination. The head-spinning effect of such turns is part and parcel of their highly controlled and simple trajectory. They are a parody of Plato's exceptional cave dweller who turns his head toward true light, to the light *of* truth, which nonetheless also belongs on the same metaphysical axis with the fire illuminating the realm of appearances.

One reason for the constant activation of our intellectual body's pivot joints is the exorbitant demand of the academic publication mill, which, under a publish-or-perish model, goes into overdrive with the trendy topics *du jour*. Another (related) reason is the ideology of innovation that treats the generation of knowledge as the production of scholarly novelty items. The fetish of the new presupposes, as its indispensable underside, the depreciation of ancient insights and worldviews. The atlantoaxial joint of our intellectual body is put to work incessantly, the head turning from left to right and from right to left, also in the political sense that often goes unacknowledged when it comes to the accelerating "turns."

...

Someone calls my name, a vague someone who, announced only by and as a voice, is not in my visual field at the moment. I turn my head in the direction of the call. That is the original scene of interpellation, signaling the birth of the subject in a densely ideological situation. Žižek observes: "Many interpreters and critics of Althusser's theory of interpellation already pointed out the circularity of the process of interpellation: yes, ideology interpellates an individual into subject; however, for the individual to recognize itself in the interpellation, it must already be open to interpellative call, i.e., in Hegelese, it must already be a subject 'in itself.'"[165] Everything here is mediated by the wheel-like joint of recognition, which puts turns and turnings in motion and which *in its turn* depends on these very turnings and turns. In the lived materiality of my interpellated body, it is the atlantoaxial joint that silently responds to the call and, in doing so, corresponds to the intention of the authority that interpellates me and to my own self-recognition in the interpellation (my being "a subject 'in itself'"). A turn of the head as turning the screw of interpretation . . .

...

In the second half of the twentieth century, Henry James's 1898 novella *The Turn of the Screw* occasioned a plethora of literary and psychoanalytic interpretations. A haunting narrative about a haunting (of children or of their governess, depending on one's perspective), the text has very little to say about the expression that serves as its title, except in the moment when the young governess reflects on the task entrusted to her. "Here at present," she recounts,

> I felt afresh—for I had felt it again and again—how my equilibrium depended on the success of my rigid will, the will to shut my eyes as tight as possible to the truth that what I had to deal with was, revoltingly, against nature. I could only get on at all by taking 'nature' into my confidence and my account, by treating my monstrous ordeal as a push in a direction unusual, of course, and unpleasant, but demanding after all, for a fair front, only another turn of the screw of ordinary human virtue. No attempt, none the less, could well require more tact than just this attempt to supply, one's self, *all* the nature.[166]

We will put to one side, for the time being, the circumstances the governess is alluding to. The tense situation in the presumably haunted household she has been incorporated into is the pretext for confronting *any* disturbing events, experienced as a "monstrous ordeal," by *anyone* whatsoever. Psychic balance turns and returns to ("again and again") the strength of the will, its rigidification, or, more precisely, to the feeling that this balance rides on such rigidity. Reexperiencing the feeling in question is not reconfirming a simple mental attachment to the ideal of a resolute will; rather, it turns in the spiral of tightening this will itself, according to the screw thread cut into the psyche. The direction of rotary movements is clear: they proceed against what is deemed to be "revoltingly" "against nature," *contra-contra-natura*. It is this direction that the governess sees as "unusual, of course, and unpleasant, but demanding after all . . . only another turn of the screw of ordinary human virtue." The unwavering commitment to virtue is driving the rigidification of the will with every turn of the screw.

What transpires with every turn of the screw of virtue? Dissociation, turning away from reality, from the world. The will must be strong enough "to shut my eyes as tight as possible to the truth [of] what I had to deal with." Unalloyed idealist maximalism always dictates that one act and think as if the world that stands in the way of the ideal did not exist. *Think and act*, it enjoins, *as if the collapse of the entire world were not as important as the possibility of upholding the high standards of virtue*; *fiat iustitia et pereat mundus*—"let justice be done, even if the world perishes" (Ferdinand I, Luther, Kant . . .). Psychic equilibrium, so understood and so practiced, is discordant with the equilibrium of the world. Should you think that what happens in external reality is against nature, you will look for being-according-to-nature in virtue, in the inner moral core, increasing the distance between yourself and that unacceptable reality with every turn of the screw. Ultimately, in the madness that ensues, you will have located the totality of nature *within*, in "this attempt to supply, one's self, *all* the nature."

The growing inflexibility of the will, of virtue, of the walls separating a maximalist subject from the world is the outcome of an action that can only be performed by a hand that turns the screw ever tighter, that is to say, by the pivot joint of the wrist, passing its own rotary movement to the screw. Here, we are dealing with an invisible hand (yes: despite being invisible, this hand also has joints)—not of the market, but of subjects, who work on *themselves*. The tightness of the screw it drives in, strengthening virtue, is the measure of repression. But in the rather obvious psychoanalytic reading of these moves it is easy to let slip a paradox, where the ensuing rigidity depends on the mobility of the pivot joint. Psychic closure and rotation on a single plane, with one degree of freedom, go literally hand-in-hand. The dynamism of inner life is responsible for its eventual stagnation or fixation, the drive getting stuck. And already the repetitive routine of reestablishing one's mental equilibrium, tied to the recurrent feeling that it "depended on the success of my rigid will," absorbs into itself the difference between the static and the dynamic, between the turns of the invisible wrist and the screw of virtue it tightens until the instant when this screw can no longer turn at all.

The final turn of the screw that proudly demonstrates the rigidity of the will and the inflexibility of virtue coincides with the rigor mortis of death. The novella's closing lines depict the governess with the boy in her care, Miles, in her arms, apparently protected from the ghost (of Peter Quint): "With the stroke of the loss I was so proud of, he [Miles] uttered the cry of a creature hurled over an abyss, and the grasp with which I recovered him might have been that of catching him in his fall. I caught him, yes, I held him—it may be imagined with what a passion; but at the end of a minute I began to feel what it truly was that I held.

We were alone with the quiet day, and his little heart, dispossessed, had stopped."[167] The grasp, as Shoshana Felman argues, is the key to this scene and to Miles's murder; it connotes the "comprehension . . . of the meaning of the Other," the secure knowledge "which constitutes the ultimate aim of any act of reading" and "is thus conceived as a violent gesture of appropriation, a gesture of domination of the Other."[168] How to read this scene—and its interpretation—from the perspective of the joints, though?

The grasp immobilizes both the hand that grasps and the object it detains. To arrest and comprehend, it has no other choice but to deaden the comprehended and itself, the barely comprehended subject of comprehension. Turns and turnings are disallowed: no becoming-other, no rotary movement of organs or parts of organs. Driven fully in, maximally tightened, the screw of interpretation feigns the superfluousness of interpretation; truth is rendered independent from the exegetical movement of thought and claims for itself the fixity of an atemporal, non-perspectival ideal.[169] Joints can be no longer told apart from bones.

...

Is it necessary to choose between incessant turnings and absolute stability? Aren't joints, among other kinds of articulation, stable and mobile, even if they are pivot joints? Whether rotating or motionless, wheels are the figures of stability: a circle is an image of eternity, of an eternal return. They roll over and level the distinction between movement and rest, unless they articulate the elements of this distinction by relieving them of tensions and downright contradictions.

...

Augustine's conversion is not a single event, marking a clear break between the before and the after, the unrepentant and repentance, falsehood and truth. It proceeds in a series of turns, returns, and counterturns enabled by the spiritual pivot joint. Augustine laments his "broken condition" of dispersion, which he attributes to being "turned away from you [God; *te adversus*]" and to squandering himself in "multiple vanities" (*Conf.* II.1).[170] Divine mercy forgives the sins of "those who turn unto you [*conversis ad te*]" (II.7).[171] The entire economy of the soul's turning is summarized between these two passages from *The Confessions*: "Thus, the soul commits fornication, when she turns from you [*avertitur ab te*], seeking those things without you, which she can nowhere find pure and untainted, till she returns again to you [*redit ad te*]. Thus, all perversely imitate you [*perverse te imitantur*], even those who get themselves far from you" (II.6).[172]

Conversion belongs on the same plane of rotary movement with perversion and an adversarial relation to God, to oneself, and to the things one really desires. The *-vers-* embedded in all three of these words is an echo of the Latin verb *vertere*, which means to "change," "become," "turn," "revolve," "exchange," "translate," "alter," "overthrow." The act of pivoting involves these multiple meanings by turns, as well as concurrently. Turning away from something is turning toward something else: turning away from God is turning toward a life of fornication and sin. Yet, turning away from God is turning toward God, whether perversely, via imitation from afar, or properly, in light of the realization that the enjoyment of anything is unfeasible without a return to the divine guarantor of existence. Turning is a movement of with-against, of conversion and aversion, of return and non-return.

But what exactly is the spiritual pivot joint? Connecting and separating "the God of revenge" and the God who is a "fountain of mercies," this joint is a "wonderous contraption," or a "miraculous means," *miris modis*, of "converting us to you [*qui convertis nos ad te*]" (*Conf.* IV.4).[173] The confessional illustration Augustine furnishes has to do with his male lover, baptized at the brink of death and brought back to life immediately afterwards. Augustine's apparently jesting offer for his friend to turn his back on his baptism was met with scorn, a discourse of "a wonderous and sudden freedom [*mirabili et repetina libertate*]," and the real possibility of the friend turning into a "mortal enemy [*inimicum*]" (IV.4).[174] Finally, the lover's fever relapses (*repetitur febribus*) and he dies, devastating Augustine, who writes that his "paternal house became a source of wonderful unhappiness [*paterna domus mira infelicitas . . . verterat*]" to him (IV.4).[175]

What I have dubbed "the spiritual pivot joint" operates a change of signs, from the positive to the negative or vice versa (this *versa* itself participating in the pivotal movement of *vertere*). Augustine's lover converts to Christianity, and the turning of his life to death is interrupted, only to be overturned and come to an abrupt end in his early demise. The death of the beloved implies that "all sweetness utterly turns [*versa*] into bitterness" (*Conf.* IV.9).[176] Before that happens, the dearest friend and object of affection threatens to turn into a mortal enemy. The miraculous combines the means of conversion and a state of freedom with misery. And God himself is converted from that of revenge to "a fountain of mercy" in a divine change of signs.

The swing from plus to minus (and back) is consistent with rotation on a single plane, which is the function of a pivot joint. The more frequently it occurs, the more this spiritual joint is put to work. Conversion, then, is a reiterated choice, which may be reaffirmed or betrayed—and sometimes, betrayed in its being reaffirmed. Facing it, we may at any moment activate the atlantoaxial joint, moving our heads from side to side: *no*.

For Augustine, this is an immense source of despair. "Why now, my perverse [*perversa*] soul," he asks, "will you still be following your own flesh? Let the flesh rather follow you now that you have converted [*ipsa te sequitur conversam*]" (*Conf.* IV.11).[177] Perversion is not only a possible betrayal of conversion; it is conversion's most intimate possibility. (Generally speaking, the most intimate possibility of a thing is its betrayal.) In addition to the rotative movement of *vertere* that fuels them both, the act of conversion needs perversion to push off against, to gain traction, and this ineradicable crookedness of the soul keeps shadowing life after that initial act. The act of turning toward God offers no guarantees that one would not turn away from him—especially if one is a *spiritus ambulans*, "a wandering spirit" (IV.15),[178] that is, a spirit with an active pivot joint perpetually ready to rotate from one side to the other on the single plane of existence allotted to it: from the creator to creation, from the one to the many, from the primacy of the soul to that of the flesh, and back. Perversion precedes and succeeds conversion, negatively impelling it as well, much like disarticulation precedes and succeeds articulation, with which it is also interspersed.

Art's Articulations

There are as many definitions of art as there are art theorists and philosophers of aesthetics. For my part, I am interested in the most obvious and superficial one, which may not be on their radars on account of its conspicuousness and banality. This definition or designation coincides with what we say whenever we utter the word "art," at least in English and in Romance languages, in which, as we have seen, joints are linguistically indistinguishable from articulations.[179]

Art articulates. By virtue of articulating, it is art. My hunch is that—regardless of its content, theme, subject matter, genre, or style—art distills the articulations and disarticulations of the world from the world. Art works on the joints of the world, but also of worlds, of one world and another, of a world and an unworld. It teases out the processes of fitting together and drawing apart that make the world what it is: a complex assemblage, where synthetic and analytic activities are physical and embodied, before some of them are sublimated into moments of human perception and cognition, which we identify with thinking *in toto*. Art as an articulation renders a human artist superfluous, because entities are articulated (they articulate themselves and join other entities) all by themselves. Heidegger's interpretation of a basic sense of the world as a totality-of-things and Benjamin's notion of "the language of things" testify to this superfluity.

Not to be outstripped, philosophers in the Western tradition have tried to remedy the situation, to re-center the human artist, by emphasizing symbolic over spatial articulations. Conventionally understood, the hierarchy of the arts passed down from Aristotle to Hegel stretches from the lowly material kinds (such as architecture) to the highest ideal varieties (such as music and poetry). Not only materiality and ideality are at stake here, or, better, these philosophical labels are at stake only as codifying the two vectors of articulation. Architecture belongs at the bottom of the hierarchy because it deals with the articulation of things in space (if not with the articulations *of* space or spaces), while music and poetry are high up on the ladder of the arts because they are concerned with the articulation of sounds and in sounds. And yet, the two moments of articulation remain, albeit on an unequal footing.

The usual temptation in the face of such hierarchies is to flip them, to place them head down. This would require elevating matter over spirit, space over time, touch over sound. Nevertheless, the convulsions of art and articulation are immanent to the same word, to the same thing that presents itself in two seemingly incompatible manners. Instead of reinventing the hierarchical head, it is imperative to chop it off, coming up with an acephalic (I would say, vegetal) configuration. Attention to articulation sustains this more radical effort. It allows us to ask, on the one hand, *how things speak*, seeing that the arrangement and distribution of phenomena in space is a form of their expression, and, on the other, *how speaking things*, given that words and sounds are already resonances with and within the places where they are emitted, with air, within the walls of a hall or among the trunks of trees in a forest.

...

"Articulation" is a beautiful word that combines two seemingly disparate significations, located on opposite sides of the barricades in the Cartesian universe. It names both a spatial jointure, assembling things in space, and an illocutionary act, creating meaning by way of expressing the world in words. That is to say, it brings together extension and intention, the real and the ideal (or the ideational). We could map the entire mind/body split, the division between the thinking thing (*res cogitans*) and the extended thing (*res extensa*), onto the different semantic inflections of "articulation." But immersing ourselves in such a cartographic endeavor, we would ascertain that the division is still a rift within the same. We should give Descartes a little more credit than we usually do. He must have known that the two share their rootstock, which is why the same noun (*res*, "thing") crops up on both sides of the Cartesian abyss. The beauty of "articulation" shines—somewhat obscurely, to be sure—through art.

...

If art says "articulation" in a condensed, concise, abbreviated form, that is because it does nothing but articulate—what? We may glimpse a partial answer in Wassily Kandinsky's 1926 book *Point and Line to Plane*.[180] There, in that text, he is more attuned to the philosophical intricacies of geometry than Hegel in the early discussion of pure space in *Philosophy of Nature*. Apropos of a point, Kandinsky specifies: "We look upon the geometric point as the ultimate and most singular union of silence and speech. The geometric point has, therefore, been given its material form in writing. It belongs to language and signifies silence."[181] The point is an articulation of speech and silence, or, in our terms, a joint of *logos*. But it can take on a plethora of geometrical shapes, including that of a square.[182] That is why Boris Groys argues that "*Black Square* (1915) by

Malevich can be interpreted as a quotation of a point on a canvas—as a sign of interruption without any indication of what it is meant to interrupt."[183] As a square-shaped point, *Black Square* is art's articulation of language and silence, of something and nothing.

As soon as one zooms out of the sonorous image of speech and silence, as Kandinsky does when discussing paintings in terms of shapes of a point, it becomes clear that these articulated extremes stand for infinitely more than what they colloquially mean. They stand for being and nothing handed over to, or withheld from, perception and understanding. So construed, they rehash the Hegelian dialectic where becoming is a double joint of these polar opposites. That is also where formal similarities to Hegelian thought end. In contrast to the dialectics of space, what becomes does so not after it has emerged from the apparent self-enclosure of a point, having been elongated into a line, but as and at a point, which marvelously morphs into lines and figures, absorbing them into itself, because, Kandinsky explains, "the point is innermost concise form."[184] Its conciseness resonates with the abbreviation of articulation in art.

Now, the innermost never stays just inner; it is merely "turned inwards" while also facing outwards.[185] Concentric and eccentric, the point-joint is Janus-faced. It is a synesthetic conversation of being and nothing, speech and silence.

Surely, art is more than a point in its various permutations. Right? It could actually be less. What art articulates is nothing (above all, in an age when the world is on the verge of becoming nothing, which is significant, assuming that art indeed distills the articulations and disarticulations of the world from the world), the nothing around which mobile joints are mobilized, the nothing which is the void of the in-between. Dancing bodies, aquarelles and charcoal, cords and wood and brass, marble and bronze and plaster (not to mention the voice, singing or speaking) are supports for the articulation of nothing—exquisitely fecund, inexhaustible in its finitude, demanding an ongoing dis- and re-articulation. In the case of art per se, rather than commercial design or political propaganda, what is on stage or on the canvas is articulation itself, the *itself* of articulation, which lacks a self amenable to being packaged in a self-contained identity and which is nothing but a relation, a fractured bond, an amalgam of continuity and discontinuity.

Starting with the theories of the beautiful and the sublime in Burke and Kant, what if it is art's articulation of nothing that mesmerizes us and draws us toward itself, magnet-like? In the sublime, the void is delimited but not entirely covered over; in the beautiful, disinterested pleasure with its own sort of negativity takes over the articulation of nothing. There is no satisfaction of desire in either of these instances, which do not, for all that, yield pure dissatisfaction. Instead, the beautiful and the sublime invite future rearticulations of the works with viewers, listeners, spectators, entire publics even, indebted to nothing, around which art builds its articulations. Kandinsky, too, obliquely endorses this interpretation. "The sound of that silence customarily connected to the point," he writes, "is so emphatic that it overshadows the other characteristics."[186]

. . .

Art's articulations excise it from the ambit of human cultural production and return it back to the world. Planetary art takes its place and time at the scale of planetary articulations. The question is not whether art as the articulation and disarticulation of the world is exclusively human. It is, rather, whether the patently human contribution is to transform art into an articulation of nothing.

...

When I write the word "nothing," I do not mean negativity, which has been a red thread running through the modern philosophy of aesthetics from Hegel to Adorno, Luhmann, Kristeva and, more recently, Artemy Magun. *Nothing* is an interval, as spatial as it is temporal, a gap, fracture, punctuation (such as a point), the inner of a cavity (such as the synovial cavity of a mobile joint) irreducible to its substance. Magun actually includes "nothingness" in the list of substantive ways in which an artwork is negative. He itemizes "the void, the nothingness, and the sheer destruction, such as Malevich's *Black Square* or John Cage's *4'33"* (active abstract negativity). But this can only be a goal, because in fact 'the nothing' is irrepresentable: if represented, it would immediately fill its own void as another object."[187] This line of reasoning holds for self-contained and discrete objects, not for articulations, joints, intrinsically broken ties, or unstable relations. Not by chance, Malevich's *Black Square* reappears in this citation, giving a clue, by juxtaposition with Kandinsky's and Groys's analyses, as to why it is not "sheer destruction." As "a sign of interruption without any indication of what it is meant to interrupt," it is the nothing removed from its delimited articulatory context and allowed to become a sign unfillable with and untraceable to another object. It is the *dis-* of disarticulation that ordains every articulation.

Magun's claim is that once represented, the nothing becomes something, the void that it was filled with an objective signification. (In effect, as soon as "nothing" is articulated with the definitive article "the," it is already something.) All articulations, however, are the articulations of something and nothing (think back to Kandinsky's speech and silence), where each extreme is the ground for the other, appearing in relation to it in the position of a figure. The interval of nothing is figured by something that surrounds it, and the substantive structures of articulation are figured by the space or the spacing, the break or the punctuation mark, around which they are arranged or in which they subsist (Plato's *chôra* comes to mind in this respect). Magun is right to infer that "it is unclear where is the chicken and where is the egg"[188] here. Art's articulation of nothing refers to both—the nothing articulated by its substantive surroundings *and* the nothing that actively articulates something around or in itself. The ambiguity of the genitive has a profound philosophical significance: a subject and an object of articulation, nothing is the figure and the ground, active and passive, articulating and articulated.

In art, as in other spheres of life-death, trouble brews in absolute disarticulation, resulting from the hypostasis of nothing, its release from the play of figure and ground, the irreparable disruption of jointures. Absolute disarticulation is the end of art and the end of life, regardless of the mimetic or representational approaches this pair has been inviting throughout history. When disarticulation waxes absolute and nothing is hypostatized, it turns into an actual negativity and is lost as nothing. There is no more interval there, only a chasm without edges, without limits, or, in the words of Ibn ʿArabī (whom we have already encountered in these pages), an ocean without a shore. Finite existence is permeated and bookended by nothing on every side; the task of articulating nothing, most dramatically posed before art, implies making room and taking time between these bookends of existence, that is, receiving space and time within the liberating confines of the interval—say, of a cosmic joint.

Short of absolute disarticulation, a meta-play of figure and ground in art may be expressed in two ways. On the one hand, disarticulation may appear as a moment of articulation, yielding the negative content of art. On the other hand, articulation may be presented as a moment of disarticulation, producing art's negative form. It is easier to swallow and digest, both experientially and critically-analytically, negative content than negative form, inasmuch as this content indicates how nothing is a point of transition from something to something, a manageable gap still tied to the dynamics of a joint. By contrast, a negative form inverts the relation of articulation and disarticulation, valorizing the latter and paving the way to absolute disarticulation. But where does all this happen?

Negative content may include tragedy, as in ancient drama, or extreme suffering and violence, as in much of Christian sacred art. A negative form, in turn, is prevalent in modernism, where "the modern" is raised to a principle, requiring a break with past aesthetic, philosophical, sociopolitical, and other forms and an unquenchable search for ever new ones. James Joyce and T. S. Eliot, Schoenberg and Stravinsky, Manet and Picasso, Le Corbusier and van der Rohe spearheaded modernist experimentation across the arts. Magun argues that the tendency of modernism is toward "deformation," in that "modernism is saturated with eschatological mood and this mood inspires it to destroy artistic form."[189] Modernism, I might add by way of a rejoinder, *creates* a negative artistic form, which is ideally dynamic and mutable. What seems to be pure destruction and deformation is an element of perpetual re-creation.

• • •

In the Western history of articulations, which is yet to be written, words and abstract signs have been consistently privileged over spatial joints, and the language of things has been all but forgotten. The nothing of art's articulation has been slotted into a semantic framework accessible to the human mind and gaze alone. Paradoxically, within this framework, it could only be identified as *something*. How to circle back to art as the articulation of nothing?

...

The Basque modernist sculptor Jorge Oteiza honed the articulation of nothing in stone, iron, and bronze, to mention only some of the materials he worked with. For example, the six-meter-tall *Empty Construction with Four Flat Negative-Positive Units, 1957*, installed in San Sebastián's Paseo Nuevo in 2002, is a masterpiece of the sculptural articulation of nothing. A complex joint interrelating the sea and the shoreline, the sky and the solar blaze above, it is particularly effective in articulating the emptiness at its heart, as well as the negative and positive axes of inexistence and existence. Unlike the Greek temple that, according to Heidegger's "The Origin of the Work of Art," "first joins together and simultaneously gathers around itself the unity of those paths and relations in which birth and death, disaster and blessing, victory and disgrace, endurance and decline obtain the form of destiny for human being,"[190] Oteiza's *Empty Construction* articulates nothing, and only by means of *this* articulation is it capable of articulating everything else.

Since Oteiza also had a robust writing practice, the articulation of nothing in his art was complete: a jointure of both modalities of articulation. According to his self-interpretation, in his sculptures Oteiza protested and moved past the heavy and "cylindrical" view of the human and of the world, which he had found, for instance, in Cézanne. The techniques the Basque sculptor employed were those of perforation and what he called "aesthetic dilation," quite evident in the *Earth and Moon* series from 1951 to 1955.

Although it lets nothing into the work and allows the work to breathe, perforation is, taken by itself, sorely insufficient: "Experimental thinking dictates that perforation must be attempted. A worm can destroy an apple. Much of what Moore does is simply a worming away at the inherited idea of a statue. A sculptor can perforate a cylinder, but neither the apple nor the cylinder have transformed their nature." That is why "it would be necessary to transform the heavy Euclidean nature of the cylinder into a weightless unity with its centers of origin on the outside (a hyperboloid?), enabling us to attempt to create empty spaces by the accumulation of units (the fusion of these weightless nuclei) in front of the contemporary experimental sculpture, in which the aesthetic and significant energy of the empty spaces is obtained by the fission of the traditional nucleus of the heavy statue."[191]

The "weightless unity" of a statue is an achievement not of perforating (or punctuating: recall here Kandinsky and Groys on Malevich) the relentless density and continuity of matter, but of the follow-up gesture, locating the "centers of origin on the outside," so that the creation is really that of empty spaces, revealed by the "accumulation of units" around them. Oteiza changes the rules of the game as far as the figure and the ground are concerned: articulations come into being by delimiting the gap of disarticulation, the edges of which they outline; that is, they come into being via nothing. While situated between substantive units, the cardinal interval of Oteiza's works is prior to them. It emanates from the outside, vibrating with energy ("significant energy of the empty spaces") and setting space itself in motion. It is a joint.

Oteiza is even more explicit in his description of the 1949 sculpture *Mother with Son Watching the Sky in Fear*. "We have conceived this monument," he writes, "as a simple and open articulation, as a formal, lightweight system in which the interior void constitutes its expressive and tragic substance."[192] Turning a cylinder into a hyperboloid, as he puts it elsewhere, and perforating the work, the sculptor produces an articulation of nothing ("simple and open"). If the interior void is constitutive, then the work and the world seen from the perspective of this aesthetic joint are seen from the perspective of the void. The articulation of nothing is both the active content ("tragic substance," as in ancient art, as well) and the form of the work, in keeping with the predominant vector of modernism.

But the most rarefied, minimalist form of the joint, which allowed Oteiza to articulate nothing, is inherent in his practice of "disoccupation." Rapidly radicalized, disoccupation yielded his final works, after which Oteiza abandoned sculpting to concentrate on pedagogy and political activism. So, *Empty Concurrence* (1956–57) is the disoccupation of a sphere, on a par with the *Ovoid Variant of the Disoccupation of a Sphere*, currently a work of public art placed in front of Bilbao's City Hall. Whereas in perforation the substantive element of the artwork is still predominant, if no longer whole, in disoccupation this element wanes, remaining only to the extent that it is needed to spotlight the void.

At the apex of disoccupation, there are the series of *Empty Boxes* and *Metaphysical Boxes* from 1957–58. The titles of the works are somewhat misleading, because rather than boxes, these are joints, articulated and disarticulated around nothing. As Oteiza reminisces:

> For the annual examination of the international artistic situation we have the two Biennials of Contemporary Art—that of São Paulo, in Brazil, and that of Venice—which are held in alternate years. The last was the one given to me, in sculpture, at the IV Biennial of São Paulo in 1957. In my experimental proposal, printed in the catalogue describing my contribution, today we can see clearly how close I was, theoretically and experimentally, to this final nothingness, which I did not succeed in intuiting completely or in isolating until the following

> year, 1958 (*Caja metafísica, número 1* [*Metaphysical box, number 1*]), when I had to acknowledge that I had concluded my work as an experimental and professional sculptor.[193]

The "final nothingness" is the interval that, simultaneously at rest and unremittingly active, articulates, disarticulates, and rearticulates surfaces, planes, and figures around itself. The end of Oteiza's "work as an experimental and professional sculptor" is, therefore, a fresh beginning, infinite in its adherence to the possibilities of the "final nothingness."

...

Within the mimetic paradigm, art is a machine for translating, signifying or re-signifying, marking or re-marking, scaling the world down to humanly manageable, graspable, expressible terms. So conceived, art distills the articulations and disarticulations of the world from the world, even when it tries to copy them with the utmost fidelity to the "original." And it also confirms that the nothing reigns supreme. The mimetic agent is the joint between the world and the rest of humanity. Only by accommodating the nothing within, only by emptying oneself, does the artist succeeds in the task of becoming a joint—and fails in succeeding (as per Walter Benjamin).

...

The intuition of Western modernism is, most often unbeknownst to it, a very ancient one. While, by and large, Abrahamic monotheisms reject *creatio ex nihilo* (creation out of nothing), in the mystical strands of Judaism, Christianity, and Islam, this idea is fundamental. In the oldest extant text of the kabbalistic tradition, *Sēfer Yəṣīrā (The Book of*

Creation), dating from the third or fourth century B.C.E., the world is created from the "ten *sefirot* [emanations] of nothingness" (I:2),[194] the highest divine emanation *ein-sof* (infinity, or, more precisely, "without end") reduced to *ein*, or "without." In the potency of their divine being, all the emanations are but the articulations of nothing, of the "without."

In the chapter on "Tiāndì" 天地 ("Heaven and Earth") of the *Zhuangzi*, the Taoist classic roughly contemporaneous with the kabbalistic *Book of Creation*, the great beginning consists of nothing (無, *wù*):

> In the great beginning, there was nothing in all the vacancy of space; there was nothing that could be named [名, *míng*]. It was in this state that there arose the first existence, still without bodily shape. From this, things could then be produced, receiving what we call their proper character. That which had no bodily shape was divided; and then without intermission there was what we call the process of conferring. [The two processes of] stopping-moving [留動, *liú dòng*] continuing, things were produced (8).[195]

Although a divine artificer, or a demiurge, is absent from both the Jewish and Chinese texts under discussion, the principle of creation (only faintly reflected in the Latin expression *ex nihilo*) is applicable to artistic making. In the *Zhuangzi*, nothing is articulated both in the continuously discontinuous process of dividing and conferring and in naming, which is inapplicable to what was in the great beginning (namely, the unnamable, where *wù*, or nothing, is a joint between the unnamable and a name). Whether in naming or in bringing into existence, the great beginning when/where "there was nothing" is not overcome; it persists as the wellspring of being, dwelling, living, and putting things to use. Articulation is forever stamped by that beginning, not least because it must articulate the inarticulate and the inarticulable—what could not be named and what had no bodily shape. *Wù* is not exhausted in any one of its articulations, nor in the sum of all articulations, but is the interval without edges, in which they take place and which inheres in them. Across its articulations, despite its apparent futurism, art moves back to the beginning with nothing, of nothing.

This conclusion resonates with chapter 11 of the Taoist classic *Daodejing* (or *Tao Te Ching*), which contemplates the conditions of possibility for usability:

> Thirty spokes held in one hub;
> —In nothing [無, *wù*] lies the cartwheel's usefulness;
> Moulding clay into pots;
> —In nothing lies the pot's usefulness;
> Chiseling doors and windows to make a room;
> —In nothing lies the room's usefulness.[196]

Artisanal activity, technical production, architecture and dwelling are the articulations of something and nothing—say, of clay and the empty space within. Ultimately, though, because usefulness depends on nothing (a clay pot being a vessel capable of receiving liquids or other entities), the something articulated with it is, itself, an articulation of nothing. When Malevich draws his *Black Square* or when Oteiza makes his metaphysical and empty boxes in line with the principle of disoccupation, they enact this interpretation, extending it beyond usefulness to the entire ontology of the art object and of the world at large.[197]

Oddly enough—and despite the logic of the articulation of nothing that it develops—the *Daodejing* rejects aesthetics, comprising the arts and the entire human sensorium, for its blindness, deafness, and overall disregard for *wù*. Programmatically, chapter 12 states:

> The five colours turn a man's eyes blind;
> The five notes turn a man's ears deaf;
> The five tastes turn a man's palate dull;
> Racing through fields hunting turns a man's heart wild;
> Goods hard to obtain cause a man's progress to halt.[198]

According to this line of reasoning, art's articulations are so luminous and overwhelming that they divert the gaze, the ear, the palate, and the heart from nothing. A more powerful diversion comes on the heels of another diversion characteristic of the senses that, by tending, by attending to their objects (seeing to the visible, hearing to the audible, etc.), get distracted from nothing. An aesthetic object lends itself to the senses in the condition of an unpardonable imbalance, stressing something over nothing with greater insistence than other kinds of objects. Overlaying and intensifying the amazing array of colors, sounds, tastes, and so on, the mediations of art effectively prevent *wù* from reaching human senses, hearts, and minds.

Functionality (用, *yòng*), which is what it is exclusively through nothing, approximates *wù* better, more completely, than beauty. Wang Bi, the third century B.C.E. commentator on the *Daodejing*, writes regarding chapter 11 of the work: "That wood, clay, and wall can form these three things [wheel, vessel, room] depends in each case on achieving functionality [用, *yòng*] through the nothing [無, *wù*]. In other words, [as for nothingness] what is there can be of benefit always depends on its achievement of functionality through what is not there."[199] All making is an articulation of nothing, of "what is there" with "what is not there." In fulfilling the requirement of usability—in being beneficial, good for something—a thing is more austere, regardless of its purely ornamental accoutrements, and, as such, it does not detract from the nothing it articulates in its form and in every use made of it. The disinterested pleasure which Kant allocates to art is an emptying-out that turns out to be neither as vacuous nor as close to nothing as the Taoist understanding of functionality.

...

To sum up, art is the play of the extensive and the intensive regimes of articulation. Otherwise stated, art is the self-consciousness of a joint. It works and plays with the nothing that is already there in the language of things (of plants, of insects, of rocks, of the elements, of the world), each of them negating itself to relate to all others and becoming itself in its self-negation. A transposition from the one to the other regime of articulation is never complete: the extensive physical jointures of objects and contexts are irreducible to the intensive and intentional regime of articulation with which they interact, *and* they contain, often in barely recognizable forms, this other regime within themselves. In art, as art, extensive and intensive articulations keep changing places, passing into one another, even passing *for* one another, only to part ways before yet another convergence. Much of art's explosive force derives from its capacity to transcribe (endlessly, daringly, erringly and erroneously) one regime of articulation into another. This transcription is the work of nothing, the nothing, which has nothing to do with strictly human realities.

...

By articulating, art acts, and it does so with a certain incontinence, ranging over the two registers of articulation and the play between them. As an articulation of nothing, art must also heed the call of nonacting (literally: "nothing-doing"), concentrated in the Taoist notion of 無為 (*wùwei*). According to the *Daodejing*'s chapter 48,

> A person given to studies makes daily increase;
> A person given to the Way makes daily diminution.
> Diminish [損, *sûn*] and again diminish,
> Until coming to not acting [無為, *wùwei*].
> When not acting then there is nothing not done.[200]

Wùwei is an articulation without articulation, a letting-articulate-and-disarticulate. The chapter of *Daodejing* where it is mentioned starts with a contrast between positive and negative poles, between increase and diminution, the art of learning and the art of unlearning. But toward the end of the chapter, *wùwei* emerges on the side of a plenitude that, by means (in part) of a double negative, exceeds the opposition of presence and absence, accomplishment and non-accomplishment: "When not acting then there is nothing not done." With this, *wùwei* is revealed as the release of the world to its own articulations and disarticulations, an acknowledgment and an embrace of the art of the world.

Non-doing is not sheer passivity, of course. Some have proposed that, by praising *wùwei*, Taoist texts endorse "the absence of purposive activity."[201] If so, then Kant's understanding of art as purposiveness without purpose, which yields disinterested pleasure, would seem to dovetail with this notion. The argument is precipitous. Purpose and function have been shown to shelter *wù* (nothing) and, therefore, are not at odds with *wùwei*; one should not brush them off that easily. So, what does non-doing mean?

As chapters 37 and 38 in the *Daodejing* indicate, *wùwei* is the activity of the Way (道), of *Tao* or *Dao*:

> The Way in its regular course does nothing [道常無為, *dào cháng wù wei*],
> And so, there is nothing which it does not do.[202]

Through the practice of *wùwei*, one joins the "regular course" of the Way. But whereas the Way itself warrants the immediate coincidence of nothing and everything (or more precisely, of absolute potency and the dissipation of potency), a human practitioner of *wùwei* must articulate not just these extremes but, at a certain meta-level, articulate the pair articulation/disarticulation and non-articulation (hence, my earlier invocation of "articulation without articulation"). The paradox is that we must pour a sustained effort into effortlessness. Years of grueling physical training are behind the spectacle of the freedom of the body, apparently hovering above the floor in dance or in high jump, where non-doing comes through in the doing. By comparison, the practice of *wùwei* is inverted. Here, occasionally, doing comes through in the non-doing, which is articulated with it in a different figure-ground relation. To join, or to rejoin, the "regular course" of the Way, we must dramatically modify the regular course of human practices that are, in their own way, the Way's regular course, as well.

Wùwei, then, is art and non-art: art as non-art and non-art as art. In the words of the *Zhuangzi*, it is heaven-like: "Acting without acting is called heavenly [無為為之之謂天]."[203] Yet, we are on earth, between heaven and earth, at a planetary, cosmic jointure. Articulation—even as meager as the articulation of nothing—is our fate. The *Zhuangzi* subtly confirms this by including the joint of heaven and earth in the otherwise "heavenly" provenance of *wùwei*: "Emptiness, stillness, limpidity, silence, nothing-doing—these are the level [平, *píng*] of heaven and earth [天地, *tiāndì*], the substance of the Way and virtue."[204] The level (平, *píng*) is the joint, the horizontality of the vertical, where what is above belongs together with what is below and is the *above* by virtue of the *below*; where separation is a connection and connection is a separation; where the art of nothing-doing and articulating nothing is everything.

The Arthritic Society

In a world with a rapidly aging population, the incidence of arthritis is on the rise. According to a recent study published in *Lancet Rheumatology*, by 2050, just shy of one billion people worldwide will be living with osteoarthritis, the most common form of the disease in adults.[205] That is nearly double the cases registered in 2020. In terms of sheer numbers alone, we are undeniably heading toward a global arthritic society.

In countries and regions with large aging populations, geriatrics is one of the priorities, and issues associated with it are among the top R&D goals. This is certainly the case in the Basque Country, throughout the Iberian Peninsula, and in Europe overall. But epidemiological population trends are only a tip of the proverbial iceberg. If all kinds of bodies (textual and political, the bodies of knowledge and thought, associations and communities, ecologies and economies) have joints, among other articulations, then the arthritic society is a future horizon for all of them as they undergo aging, wear and tear, and, worse, the "abnormal remodeling of joint tissues driven by a host of inflammatory mediators,"[206] now recognized as a prominent cause of osteoarthritis. Depending on the kind of body in question, its arthritic syndrome will be expressed differently. Let me, in a very schematic manner, outline how this syndrome affects the bodies of thought, politics, and textual traditions.

...

In many Slavic languages, the word for *joint* begins with the prefix "with" (*s*-, *su*-). The Bulgarian *stava*, the Slovenian *sklèp*, the Ukrainian *suhlob*, the Russian *sustav*, and the Belorussian *sustau* are some of the examples of this semantic arthrology. The being of joints is being-with. That which hurts in arthritis of any kind is the *with*. What remains in cases of extreme articular damage is a state (status, stance, stature: **sta*) without joints or gaps, the totalitarian state of being without the *with*.

...

Once we accept that ideas are not the immortal and immaterial entities they were once deemed to be—that is to say, once we take seriously the thesis that ideas come into being, age, and pass away—the implication is that, in the period of their decline, they start getting frayed around the edges and tear at the seams or break up at the sutures. Budding, blossoming, ripening, decaying, and fermenting are the vegetal images for the aging of ideas in Hegel's dialectics. Their animal deterioration is less elegant than that. Eidetic arthralgia may ensue.

What, then, hurts when the joints of ideas are inflamed or otherwise debilitated?

To begin with, what hurts are the connections and separations among the ideas themselves. When the mediations between them wear thin, friction is inevitable. These mediations include language—both natural and conceptual languages. Ideas originally expressed in ancient Greek and in Latin are barely articulable in modern languages (also because, as Heidegger would say, they are conceptual wrecks that have outlived their world). But one need not go so far back in history: in the twenty-first century, the continental and analytic traditions do not speak the same conceptual language, triggering an eidetic arthralgia in philosophy.

It is actually a mistake to consider a consistent body of thought to be immobile, monumentally static, or eternally selfsame. The articulations of ideas are fragile, yet freeing; they are the points of severe stress as much as of liberating possibilities. Thought moves. Ideas circulate, articulate and are articulated, often through their inner contradictions, bespeaking their non-fused nature. Arthritic affliction flares up when the inner contradictions in a system of ideas are no longer hidden, when they explode, threatening that system as a whole. Philosophers have put forth several models to explain the fate of aging thought: a series of metamorphoses, the birth of new ideas (and worlds) from the decaying bodies of the old ones, the progress of enlightened reason gradually breaking with the darkness of ignorance and leaving prejudices behind, or the recycling of the long-forgotten past of thought in ostensibly new forms. Arthrosophy has its own contribution to make: the history of metaphysics as a protocol for spiritual hip replacement surgeries.

Even when it comes to ideas, the sites of affliction are the joints of time. If philosophy is the child of its time—the time which it manages to comprehend in thought—then it belongs in the caesura opened up by that time. The synovial cavity of ideas is shaped by their dated and emplaced contexts, traditions, and languages in which they emerge. A lack of fit between the spatiotemporal synovial cavity and the ideational joint it houses causes abrasions, pain, and swelling. The ideal of immutable being, inherited by Greek philosophy from Egyptian thought, does not correspond to ecological thought and action. Metaphysical philosophy is chronically arthritic; it never fits comfortably in its synovial time-joints, in that it aims to abolish time as such or, at the very least, depreciates temporal existence and tries to break with the world once and for all.

However out of joint or afflicted by ontological arthritis they may be, the joints of time are the links between thinking and being, between ideas and *what is*. Temporal through and through, Hegelian dialectics is the permanent irritation of this connection, seeking the cure for its arthritis in the rational becoming actual and in the actual becoming rational. Adorno's negative dialectics accepts and, with sadomasochistic flare, revels in the non-coincidences, non-identities, and arthritic symptomatology of thought and the world, each in itself and each in its relation to the other—this is the gist of his "critique of positive negation."[207] But the time-joints articulating thought and the world also suffer from arthritic conditions that are not, properly speaking, dialectical.

Aside from wear and tear, abnormal tissue remodeling accounts for osteoarthritis, understood as "a 'whole joint disease,' with all joint tissues, including the cartilage, subchondral bone, and so on being involved in pathogenesis."[208] In their contact with reality, ideas can also undergo abnormal remodeling, infiltrating, often without anyone noticing, everyday life beyond the sphere of common sense. Metaphysical ideas and ideals of the unchangeable live on, unrecognized, in this arthritic relation between thought and reality. They change, assuming the material form of non-decomposable artifacts that clog ecosystems: spent nuclear fuel rods, plastics and "forever chemicals," heavy metals and the like. Or, on the contrary, ideas may be deemed useless (or even counterproductive), irreconcilable with the overtly stated purposes of a society or a particular class. Upon coming into contact with life engineered in this way, they may undergo abnormal remodeling due to the overwhelming demands of technical applicability and political subservience. It is then that some of the ideas will be remodeled into an ideology.

...

Ideology = the arthritic *logos* of ideas.

...

Political arthritis is the fate of regimes on the verge of losing their vitality, growing oblivious to the movements (often of a revolutionary kind) that installed and legitimated them, and getting buried under piles of bureaucracy. The "end of history" Francis Fukuyama declared in the 1990s was a harbinger of "degenerative" or "mechanical" political arthritis. Fukuyama's triumph lasted for a very short period—either until the events of 9/11 or until the rise of the far right in the West and, especially, until the invasion of Ukraine by Russia under Putin's leadership, first in 2014 and on a larger scale in 2022. A double tragedy is that the end of the end does not automatically spell out a new beginning. The reinvigoration of a political community is a difficult matter, and arthritis often does not leave room for the regeneration of damaged tissues and organs, which is why the lackluster and puzzled responses to the return of intense contention, enmity, and war have themselves been largely arthritic.

Carl Schmitt's theoretical framework yields a high-resolution X-ray image of political arthritis. If political existence bubbles up in tensions between friend and enemy groupings, then the apparently painless situation of not having any enemies is a symptom of the onset of arthritic degradation. As a joint, the friend-enemy distinction is an articulation assembled around disarticulation, a break, a discontinuity, and it draws its sense from these forms of rupture. The intensification of the distinction may lend actuality to the possibility of war (be it internal, civil, or external, global or hybrid), while its weakening contributes to the degradation of politics. As Schmitt writes with regard to the intensification: "The enemy is negated otherness. But this negation is mutual and this mutuality of negations has its own concrete existence, as a relation between enemies; this relation of two nothingnesses on both sides bears the danger of war."[209] Its obverse is depoliticization, which, rather than an actual dissipation of the friend-enemy distinction, is its repression, its expulsion from the sphere of public consciousness to the obscurity of the unconscious.

The point is that the flare-ups of political arthritis make themselves felt in both scenarios, in the intensification and in the weakening of friend-enemy confrontations. In addition to "mechanical degradation" and joint wear and tear in apparently depoliticized political regimes, reactive arthritis may set in. This malady is instigated by a response to the enemy as an "infection," in light of Roberto Esposito's immunological paradigm, where community is "co-immunity."[210] The reception of the other in general as an infectious agent to be purged from the body politic—the negative reception, therefore, that insists on the uncompromising rejection and physical ejection of the other from the space of a political community—triggers reactive arthritis, debilitating articulations, stiffening the political joints and forcing them to blend with osseous structures. For, when it comes to joints, strength and weakness do not boast the usual connotations. Their strength lies in affording the body its mobility—hence, in what from the standpoint of fundamental stability is deemed weak, a crucial factor in rendering an articulated body fragile.

Political articulations are subject to further undermining when one of their significations becomes hegemonic (that is, when they are "sutured" to only one of their senses, as Badiou puts it). Most often, articulation taken in terms of verbal and ideational expression predominates over its spatial connotations. In the field of political philosophy, Chantal Mouffe refashions Schmitt's figure of the enemy into a debating adversary in liberal democracy at the expense of a real confrontation. "The democratic logic of constituting the people," Mouffe writes,

> and inscribing rights and equality into practices, is necessary to subvert the tendency towards abstract universalism inherent in liberal discourse. But the *articulation* with the liberal logic allows us constantly to challenge—through reference to 'humanity' and the polemical use of 'human rights'—the forms of exclusion that are necessarily inscribed in the political practice. . . . Notwithstanding the ultimate contradictory nature of the two logics, their *articulation* therefore has very positive consequences, and there is no reason to share Schmitt's pessimistic verdict concerning liberal democracy.[211]

The articulation Mouffe describes has to do with "the two logics"—the liberal logic and the one challenging it to be more inclusive than it is—such that the political arena is a place, or a non-place, for the battle of ideas, or, to be honest, of one idea against a slightly more dogmatic version of itself. The constituting and constituted people has no body; its body politic is a polemical dialogue of two logics, unless it is one and the same internally articulated logic locked in a self-confrontation. Regardless of its radicality, liberal theory is the rheumatoid arthritis of political thought and actuality, the immune system attacking the body's own tissues at the joints and eating away at their material, embodied articulations.

At the other extreme, totalitarian systems of governance decimate the officially recognized structures and organizations of civil society. In doing so, they destroy the buffer zone between individuals and families, on the one hand, and the state, on the other. An internally fractured, articulated body politic moves with greater degrees of freedom, compared to the totalitarian system that directly subjects the individual to the power of the state and aims to re-create this body, at best, in the image of a slug. Defying common sense and the principle of noncontradiction, a functional democracy *is* brokenness, a method of constituting and reconstituting the polity at the joints, left open, visible, exposed, vulnerable. And a functional totalitarian system not only lacks any joints, but also endeavors to transform this lack into a source of its strength.

Suffice it to glance at the formal outline of Hegel's *Philosophy of Right* (and Hegel is by no means a democrat!), where civil society plays the role of a necessary mediation, to get the hang of political arthrology. In its absence, the state bears down with the full weight of its apparatus on private actors, a condition that is as oppressive as it is arthritic, with the members of the body politic and that very body rubbing directly against one another. Even so, the experience of totalitarian systems shows that civil society does not disappear altogether. It is replaced by thick, informal support networks, many of them not registering on the radars of the authorities. Plagued by political arthritis, the articulations may regenerate elsewhere—for instance, after retreating underground and forging alternative connections in the manner of roots.

...

Damóxenus of Athens (fourth century B.C.E.) was an ancient Greek comic poet, the author of at least two plays mentioned and cited at length by Athenaeus of Naucrates.[212] One of Damóxenus's plays, titled *Syntrophoi*, contains the parodic attribution of a certain insight to the pre-Socratic philosopher Democritus. Among the lines of this work are the following: "Of balanced humors everything consists [*eis . . . ho chumos homalôs pantachoû sunístatai*]. / Hence, says Democritus, the things that come into being are inevitably eaten up by arthritis [*ou dei pragmata ginomena . . . ton phagont' arthritikon*]" (Damoxen, Fr. 2, *Syntrophoi* III, 102b).[213] Damóxenus postulates, if jokingly, the imbalance of the humors as the cause of arthritis. But every joke has a grain of truth. The joints are not only joints; they include every relation holding the bodies of finite beings together. To be "eaten up by arthritis," *ton phagont' arthritikon*, is to drop out of the meshwork of relations that make one who one is. It is to return to the dispersion of isolated atoms, which is why the name of Democritus comes in handy.

...

Religious, philosophical, and cultural traditions have been getting a bad press since the dawn of modernity. Bacon's recommendation to smash the idols of the past and Descartes's doubt prompting him to do away with every established certainty except for that of the *cogito* have cast all "received knowledge" in a negative light. For the philosophers of early modernity, tradition was the realm of stagnation, a suffocating and mystifying veil that had to be torn and destroyed for human emancipation to stand a chance. Against traditions of every stripe, they sought to start afresh from a blank page unburdened by the past, from what is given and received solely by and from oneself.

It doesn't take a very deep analysis to realize that theirs is a cartoon-like view of tradition. Because oral wisdom and knowledge written in the form of texts are passed on from one generation to another, the body of tradition moves; it is not at all static. This body should be seen within the panorama of time, rather than space, in which no single text or oral narrative stays the same. The joints of a tradition's body are the moments and lines of transmission, translation, and reinterpretation. Shuttled across these lines, something is lost, other bits are preserved, and still others are maintained in a transformed state. The combination of continuity and discontinuity is the basic structure of a joint, which tradition itself aspires to represent in its *inter-temporal* movement, delivering the past to the future or deriving the future from the past.

By doing away with tradition, modernity dares to carve *history* at its joints (to borrow an expression from Plato and Zhuang Zhou), to cut the transmission lines extending, with the inevitable breaks and interruptions, from the past to the present. But a living tradition, too, can suffer from arthritis, when, for example, the weight of accruing exegetical materials is so immense that it immobilizes its body, prevents reception in the midst of receptive zeal, and exerts ever increasing pressure on its joints.

When, in works such as *Analyses Concerning Active and Passive Syntheses*, Edmund Husserl deals with the sedimentation (*Sedimentierung*) of experience, he resorts to a geological term to describe the deadening force of growth, development, and temporal unfolding, in a word, of life itself in its objective products: "Every accomplishment of the living present, that is, every accomplishment of sense or of the object becomes sedimented in the realm of the dead, or rather, the dormant horizonal sphere, precisely in the manner of a fixed order of sedimentation: while at the head, the living process receives new, original life, at the feet, everything that is, as it were, in the final acquisition of the retentional synthesis, becomes steadily sedimented."[214] This process becomes acute within the cumulative experience of a tradition, where "the realm of the dead" is not a metaphorical term for experience, which has ebbed away from our living perceptual present, but the actual realm of dead authors and artists, of works that have outlived the worlds wherein they were created, of images, ideas, texts, and artifacts that turn either into fetishes or into a more or less undifferentiated mass of cultural heritage.

Perhaps, an arthrological term is preferable to the geological one, which Husserl favored to describe this process. The "fixed order of sedimentation" is external and inorganic, whereas arthritic afflictions are those of an articulated living body. Among these, gout stands out, a type of arthritis that is "a deposition disease, and is therefore defined as the presence of monosodium urate crystals (MSUCs) in tissues, most commonly in articular and periarticular structures such as cartilage, tendons, and synovial membranes of joints and bursae."[215] Painful crystallization at the joints, the accumulation of mineral, inorganic elements in parts of an organism where they do not belong, is more fitting as a diagnosis of arthritic traditions. With a single proviso: pain is a reminder that something is amiss in the hardening of structures which should be flexible, while sedimentation covers the living impulse over in such a way that the covering-over is itself covered over, inaccessible to consciousness.

The arthritis of tradition exceeds the scope of texts and their interpretations. The locus of concern in our arthritic societies is meaning itself—not the meaning that was crystal-clear and glaring at some point in history only to be lost (this conservative lament is as inane as the uncompromising opposition to tradition), but meanings yet to be found, those that, signaled in the past, beckon from the future, finite yet inexhaustible. They are the meanings that are virtually indistinguishable from the senses of existence and that announce themselves as lacunae, either viscerally painful or inspiring an ongoing search. In the worst-case scenario, the question of meaning is met with a shrug of indifference under a strong cultural anesthesia, which converts the gout of traditions and the cut of modernity into the geological forces of sedimentation.

...

In an arthritic society, where ideational, political, textual, and other joints undergo debilitation, stiffening, inflammation, and chronic degradation, there is no task more urgent than to care for and to cure articulations. Carving reality at its joints will spell out an unmitigated disaster, unless one responds to this act by mending the world at its joints. Looming large, standing in the way of the task as it appears within the confines of the present study, is nihilism—the arthritis of spirit, including of spirit conjugated and coeval with matter. Behind the scenes of its pompous definitions, nihilism is the massive breakdown of articulations, leading to objective non-differentiation and subjective indifference. *Arthrosophy* is a medicine against nihilism. Apply it daily and nightly, in generous doses, and keep the joints of meaning working.

Notes

1 Jean-Luc Nancy, *Corpus*, trans. Richard Rand (New York: Fordham University Press, 2008), 5.

2 In this sense, the lament of Elizabeth Grosz about the body remaining "a conceptual blind spot in both mainstream Western philosophical thought and contemporary feminist theory" is justifiable, but in and of itself, it is insufficient (Elizabeth Grosz, *Volatile Bodies: Toward a Corporeal Feminism* [Bloomington: Indiana University Press, 1994], 3). Likewise, Judith Butler's jump from "matter" to "body" in a cursory reading of Aristotle is too abrupt; the two are not at all synonymous. "In Aristotle," Butler writes, "we find no clear phenomenal distinction between materiality and intelligibility, and yet for other reasons Aristotle does not supply us with the kind of 'body' that feminism seeks to retrieve" (Judith Butler, *Bodies That Matter: On the Discursive Limits of "Sex"* [New York: Routledge, 1993], 33). Joints—conceptual and material, grammatical and corporeal—can provide the much-needed mediations here.

3 On the connection between *organ* and *ergon* ("work"), see Michael Marder, *Hegel's Energy: A Reading of "The Phenomenology of Spirit"* (Evanston, IL: Northwestern University Press, 2021); and Michael Marder, *The Phoenix Complex: A Philosophy of Nature* (Cambridge, MA: MIT Press, 2023).

4 This fissure between the abstract and the concrete is, itself, not abstract; it is ensconced in the disparate logics of organisms, above all the animal and the vegetal. For Hegel, the abstract whole is a characteristic of plant being, which falls apart into a multiplicity of replicated and detachable organs due to its insufficiently self-negated (hence, self-determined and internally interrelated) character: "The vegetable in fact expresses merely the simple concept of the organism, its *moments undeveloped* [*Der vegetabilische drückt auch in der Tat nur den einfachen Begriff des Organismus aus, der seine Momente* nicht entwickelt]" (*PhG* §265). All citations from Hegel's *Phenomenology*, abbreviated as *PhG*,

are my translations of G. W. F. Hegel, *Phänomenologie des Geistes*, vol. 3 of *Werke* (Frankfurt am Main: Suhrkamp, 1970).

5 Gaston Bachelard, *La Terre et les rêveries de la volonté* (Paris: Corti, 1947), 24.

6 Herbert Srebnik, *Concepts in Anatomy* (New York: Kluwer/Springer, 2002), 121.

7 On a view from the middle represented by a germinating seed, see Michael Marder, "In the Middle: Vegetal Mediations," in *Woven in Vegetal Fabric: On Plant Becomings*, ed. Charles Rouleau (Luxembourg: Casino Luxembourg, 2022), 152–77. For a view of a voyage from the middle suspended between departure and destination points, see Michael Marder, *Philosophy for Passengers* (Cambridge, MA: MIT Press, 2022).

8 William Paley, *Natural Theology*, ed. Matthew D. Eddy and David Knight (Oxford: Oxford University Press, 2008), 62.

9 Claudia Baracchi, *Aristotle's Ethics as First Philosophy* (Cambridge: Cambridge University Press, 2008), 11–12.

10 For more on the above-mentioned features of the categories, see Michael Marder, *Political Categories: Thinking Beyond Concepts* (New York: Columbia University Press, 2019).

11 Aristotle, *Parts of Animals, Movement of Animals, Progression of Animals*, trans. A. L. Peck, Loeb Classical Library (Cambridge, MA: Harvard University Press, 1937), 442. Henceforth cited in the text as *PA*.

12 Richard F. Loeser et al., "Osteoarthritis: A Disease of the Joint as an Organ," *Arthritis & Rheumatism* 64, no. 6 (June 2012): 1697–1707.

13 Jacques Derrida, *Of Grammatology*, trans. G. C. Spivak (Baltimore, MD: Johns Hopkins University Press, 1997), 65.

14 Derrida, *Of Grammatology*, 279.

15 Aristotle, *Parts of Animals*, 510–11.

16 Jean-Luc Nancy, *Derrida, Supplements*, trans. Anne O'Byrne (New York: Fordham University Press, 2023), 10.

17 "Since supplicatory gestures are numerous, scholars needed some way to group them and make them eligible for *Kontaktmagie*. They especially needed to link clasping the knees, the gesture commonly used to address a person, and clasping an altar, the other common gesture" (F. S. Naiden,

Ancient Supplication [Oxford: Oxford University Press, 2006], 10).

18 Srebnik, *Concepts in Anatomy*, 121.

19 Loeser et al., "Osteoarthritis," 1697.

20 G. W. F. Hegel, *Philosophy of Nature: Encyclopedia of the Philosophical Sciences*, part 2, trans. A. V. Miller (Oxford: Oxford University Press, 2004), 359.

21 Giorgio Agamben, *Language and Death: The Place of Negativity*, trans. Karen Pinkus and Michael Hardt (Minneapolis: University of Minnesota Press, 1982), 85.

22 Todd Cameron Thacker, "*Jie*," in *Routledge Encyclopedia of Confucianism*, ed. Xinzhong Yao (London: Routledge, 2003), 296.

23 Sigmund Freud, *Civilization and Its Discontents*, in *The Standard Edition of the Complete Psychological Works of Sigmund Freud*, vol. 21, trans. and ed. James Strachey (London: Vintage, 2001), 90–91. Henceforth *SE* refers to the *Standard Edition* of Freud's writings, followed by the volume and page numbers.

24 "*Arthron*," in *A Greek-English Lexicon*, ed. Henry George Liddell and Robert Scott, rev. Sir Henry Stuart Jones (Oxford: Clarendon, 1940).

25 Aristotle, *Historia animalium*, trans. D'Arcy Wentworth (Oxford: Clarendon, 1910), 188.

26 Srebnik, *Concepts in Anatomy*, 123.

27 Plato, *Euthyphro, Apology, Crito, Phaedo, Phaedrus*, trans. Harold North Fowler, Loeb Classical Library (Cambridge, MA: Harvard University Press, 1914), 528–29. Henceforth references to the *Phaedrus* are abbreviated as *Ph*.

28 Immanuel Kant, *Critique of Pure Reason (The Cambridge Edition of the Works of Immanuel Kant)*, ed. and trans. Paul Guyer and Allen W. Wood (Cambridge: Cambridge University Press, 1999), 691. All references to the *Critique of Pure Reason* are abbreviated as *CPR*, with the pagination of the first (A) or second (B) editions.

29 Plato, *Euthyphro, Apology, Crito, Phaedo, Phaedrus*, 534–35. For a perceptive analysis of this passage, see Holly Moore, "Animal Sacrifice in Plato's Later Methodology," in *Plato's Animals*, ed. Jeremy Bell and Michael Naas (Bloomington: Indiana University Press, 2015), 180ff.

30 Zhuangzi, *Basic Writings*, trans. Burton Watson (New York: Columbia University Press, 2003), 46.

31 For more on the treatment of the Chinese *ding*, see Michael Marder, *Pyropolitics in a World Ablaze* (Lanham, MD: Rowman and Littlefield, 2020), esp. the final chapter on "political kitchens."

32 Zhuangzi, *Basic Writings*, 33.

33 Zhuangzi, *Basic Writings*, 46.

34 Zhuangzi, *Basic Writings*, 15.

35 Plato, *Euthyphro, Apology, Crito, Phaedo, Phaedrus*, 534–35.

36 Plato, *Euthyphro, Apology, Crito, Phaedo, Phaedrus*, 534–35.

37 Plato, *Euthyphro, Apology, Crito, Phaedo, Phaedrus*, 522–23.

38 Aristotle, *Metaphysics*, vol. 1, trans. Hugh Tredennick, Loeb Classical Library (Cambridge, MA: Harvard University Press, 1975), 229.

39 Aristotle, *The Categories, On Interpretation, Prior Analytics*, trans. Harold P. Cooke, Loeb Classical Library (Cambridge, MA: Harvard University Press, 1938), 36–37.

40 Aristotle, *Poetics*, trans. Stephen Halliwell, Loeb Classical Library (Cambridge, MA: Harvard University Press, 1995), 98–99.

41 Aristotle, *Poetics*, 100–101.

42 Patrizia Laspia, *From Biology to Linguistics: The Definition of Arthron in Aristotle's Poetics* (Cham, Switz.: Springer, 2018), xii.

43 Laspia, *From Biology to Linguistics*, 23.

44 Laspia, *From Biology to Linguistics*, 32.

45 Martin Heidegger, *Beiträge zur Philosophie—vom Ereignis*, vol. 65 of *Gesamtausgabe* (Berlin: Vittorio Klostermann, 2003), 4.

46 Heidegger, *Beiträge*, 14.

47 Heidegger, *Beiträge*, 45.

48 Agamben, *Language and Death*, 85.

49 Heidegger, *Beiträge*, 275–76.

50 Heidegger, *Beiträge*, 83.

51 Heidegger, *Beiträge*, 81.

52 Heidegger, *Beiträge*, 81. In *The Event* (trans. Richard Rojcewicz [Bloomington: Indiana University Press, 2013]), Heidegger writes, along similar lines: "Dispensation [*Fügung*] is an ordaining [*Fügen*] as event of the structure [*Gefüge*] of the time-space of the abyss, is integration [*Sich-fügen*] into the junction [*Fug*] of the beginning. The

integrative ordaining essentially occurs in the junction" (121). The "time-space of the abyss" is none other than the disjunction of the junction, the open space (for instance, the synovial cavity) of the joint.

53 Heidegger, *Beiträge*, 81.

54 Srebnik, *Concepts in Anatomy*, 129, 215.

55 Srebnik, *Concepts in Anatomy*, 215. See also Paley on this: "The joint at the *shoulder* compared with the joint at the *hip*, though both ball-and-socket joints, discover a difference in their form and proportions, well suited to the different offices which the limbs have to execute. [. . . At the lower limb the joint is endowed] with a capacity for motion, in all directions indeed, as at the shoulder, both but not to the same extent as in the arm [. . . due to a greater demand for] stability, or resistance to dislocation" (Paley, *Natural Theology*, 65).

56 Umberto Eco, *On the Shoulders of Giants*, trans. Alastair McEwen (Cambridge, MA: Belknap Press of Harvard University Press, 2019), 10–11.

57 John of Salisbury quoted in Eco, *On the Shoulders of Giants*, 11.

58 Srebnik, *Concepts in Anatomy*, 129.

59 Jean Améry, *At the Mind's Limits: Contemplations by a Survivor of Auschwitz and Its Realities*, trans. Sidney Rosenfeld and Stella Rosenfeld (Bloomington: Indiana University Press, 1980), 28.

60 Améry, *At the Mind's Limits*, 32.

61 Améry, *At the Mind's Limits*, 34.

62 Paley, *Natural Theology*, 63.

63 Améry, *At the Mind's Limits*, 28.

64 Améry, *At the Mind's Limits*, 36.

65 Améry, *At the Mind's Limits*, 36.

66 "Sash," in *An Etymological Dictionary of the English Language*, ed. Walter W. Skeat (Oxford: Clarendon, 1888), 526.

67 Jesús Rodríguez-Velasco, *Order and Chivalry: Knighthood and Citizenship in Late Medieval Castile* (Philadelphia: University of Pennsylvania Press, 2016), 4–5.

68 "Originally, the *ordo* was like a contract, allowing for pacification" (Rodríguez-Velasco, *Order and Chivalry*, 4).

69 Rodríguez-Velasco, *Order and Chivalry*, 141.

70 Rodríguez-Velasco, *Order and Chivalry*, 147.

71 Émile Benveniste, *Le Vocabulaire des institutions indo-européennes*, 2 vols. (Paris: Minuit, 1969), 99–101.

72 Arthur Green, "Introduction," in *The Zohar*, Pritzker Edition, vol. 1, trans. Daniel C. Matt (Stanford, CA: Stanford University Press, 2018), lviii.

73 All citations from the *Zohar* refer to *The Zohar*, Pritzker Edition (12 vols.), trans. Daniel C. Matt (Stanford, CA: Stanford University Press, 2018).

74 In this, they correspond to *kapha*, one of the three biological humors (*doshas*) in Ayurveda. "Kapha is wet, cold, heavy, slow, sticky, soft and firm in qualities. It gives stability, lubrication, holding together of the joints, and such qualities as patience, calm and devotion" (David Frawley, *Hindu and Vedic Knowledge for the Modern Age* [Twin Lakes, WI: Lotus, 1990], 38).

75 Luce Irigaray, *Speculum of the Other Woman*, trans. Gillian Gill (Ithaca, NY: Cornell University Press, 1985), 253.

76 Irigaray, *Speculum of the Other Woman*, 254.

77 Irigaray, *Speculum of the Other Woman*, 254.

78 Irigaray, *Speculum of the Other Woman*, 244.

79 Empedocles, *Extant Fragments*, ed. M. R. Wright (New Haven, CT: Yale University Press, 1981), 211; G. S. Kirk and J. E. Raven, *The Presocratic Philosophers: A Critical History with a Selection of Texts* (Cambridge: Cambridge University Press, 1963), 336.

80 Empedocles, *Extant Fragments*, 212; Kirk and Raven, *The Presocratic Philosophers*, 337.

81 Empedocles, *Extant Fragments*, 212–13; Kirk and Raven, *The Presocratic Philosophers*, 337.

82 Kirk and Raven, *The Presocratic Philosophers*, 328.

83 M. David Litwa, *Posthuman Transformation in Ancient Mediterranean Thought: Becoming Angels and Demons* (Cambridge: Cambridge University Press, 2021), 39.

84 DK 31, A28. Kirk and Raven, *The Presocratic Philosophers*, 329–30.

85 Empedocles, *Extant Fragments*, 166; Kirk and Raven, *The Presocratic Philosophers*, 326.

86 The earliest use of the word "cathexis" by Freud is in his studies on hysteria. See Sigmund Freud, *Studies on Hysteria*, vol. 2 of *The Standard Edition of the Complete Psychological*

Works of Sigmund Freud, trans. and ed. James Strachey (London: Vintage, 2001), 89.

87 Melanie Klein, *The Selected Melanie Klein*, ed. Juliet Mitchell (New York: Free Press, 1986), 126.

88 D. W. Winnicott, *Through Pediatrics to Psychoanalysis* (New York: Basic Books, 1975), 330.

89 Winnicott, *Through Pediatrics to Psychoanalysis*, 330.

90 Winnicott, *Through Pediatrics to Psychoanalysis*, 88.

91 Hans-Georg Schaible, "Spinal Mechanisms Contributing to Joint Pain," in *Osteoarthritic Joint Pain*, ed. Derek J. Chadwick and Jamie Goode (New York: Wiley, 2004), 5.

92 It might be tempting to dismiss Freud's studies on hysteria with the usual point about Victorian repression and the social construction of womanhood at the time, but Freud's own text refutes feminist critique. "The frequency of female hysteria," he writes, "is over-estimated; the majority of the women feared to be hysterical by physicians are strictly speaking merely neurasthenic." In turn, the "combination [of hysteria and neurasthenia] is found most frequently in hysterical men" (*SE* 1: 53).

93 D. W. Winnicott, *The Collected Works of D.W. Winnicott, Vol. 7: 1964–1966*, ed. Leslie Caldwell and Helen Taylor Robinson (Oxford: Oxford University Press, 2017), 383.

94 Winnicott, *Collected Works*, 7: 384.

95 See "Rheumatism in Children" (1929), as well clinical notes on "Rheumatic Fever," "The Rheumatic Clinic," and "The Heart, with Special Reference to Rheumatic Carditis" (1931), among others in D. W. Winnicott, *The Collected Works of D.W. Winnicott, Vol. 1: 1911–1938*, ed. Leslie Caldwell and Helen Taylor Robinson (Oxford: Oxford University Press, 2017).

96 D. W. Winnicott, *The Collected Works D.W. Winnicott, Vol. 3: 1946–1951*, ed. Leslie Caldwell and Helen Taylor Robinson (Oxford: Oxford University Press, 2017), 43–44.

97 All hymns drawn from the *Rigveda* refer to the following edition: *The Rigveda: The Earliest Religious Poetry of India*, trans. Stephanie W. Jamison and Joel P. Brereton (Oxford: Oxford University Press, 2014), 506. Henceforth this edition will be cited in text as *RV*.

98 Vidhata Mishra, *A Critical Study of Sanskrit Phonetics* (Varanasi: Chowkhamba Sanskrit Series Office, 1972), 95.

99 *The Rigveda*, 1645.
100 *The Rigveda*, 1553.
101 *The Rigveda*, 1039.
102 *The Rigveda*, 1043.
103 *The Rigveda*, 1129.
104 All hymns drawn from the *Atharvaveda* refer to the following edition: *Hymns of the Atharva-Veda* (together with extracts from the ritual books and the commentaries), trans. Maurice Bloomfield (Delhi: Motilal Banarsidass, 1973), 20. References in text to the *Atharvaveda* are abbreviated as *AV*.
105 *Hymns of the Atharva-Veda*, 45.
106 *Hymns of the Atharva-Veda*, 61.
107 Gregory P. Fields, *Religious Therapeutics: Body and Health in Yoga, Ayurveda, and Tantra* (Albany, NY: SUNY Press, 2001), 24.
108 *Hymns of the Atharva-Veda*, 194.
109 *Hymns of the Atharva-Veda*, 194.
110 Srebnik, *Concepts in Anatomy*, 124.
111 Srebnik, *Concepts in Anatomy*, 124.
112 C. Kupffer et al., "Quarterly Report on Progress in Neurology," *American Journal of Neurology and Psychiatry*, vol. 1 (1882): 289.
113 Sebastian Harth et al., "Estimating Age by Assessing the Ossification Degree of Cranial Sutures with the Aid of Flat-Panel-CT," *Legal Medicine*, vol. 11, supp. 1 (April 2009): S186–89.
114 Don Cohen, *An Introduction to Craniosacral Therapy: Anatomy, Function and Treatment* (Berkeley, CA: North Atlantic Books, 1995), 29.
115 Cohen, *An Introduction to Craniosacral Therapy*, 29.
116 Cohen, *An Introduction to Craniosacral Therapy*, 29.
117 Jacques Lacan, *The Seminar of Jacques Lacan: The Four Fundamental Concepts of Psychoanalysis (Book XI)*, ed. Jacques-Alain Miller, trans. Alan Sheridan (New York: W.W. Norton, 1998), 22 [24].
118 Lacan, *The Four Fundamental Concepts of Psychoanalysis*, 22 [25].
119 Lacan, *The Four Fundamental Concepts of Psychoanalysis*, 23 [26], translation modified.
120 "*Die Wunden des Geistes heilen, ohne daß Narben bleiben* [The wounds of the spirit heal and leave no scars behind]" (Hegel, *PhG* §669).

121 Lacan, *The Four Fundamental Concepts of Psychoanalysis*, 117 [107].
122 Lacan, *The Four Fundamental Concepts of Psychoanalysis*, 118 [107].
123 Alain Badiou, *Manifesto for Philosophy (Followed by Two Essays)*, trans. Norman Madarasz (Albany, NY: SUNY Press, 1999), 61.
124 Badiou, *Manifesto for Philosophy*, 62.
125 Badiou, *Manifesto for Philosophy*, 116.
126 Badiou, *Manifesto for Philosophy*, 64.
127 Badiou, *Manifesto for Philosophy*, 66.
128 Badiou, *Manifesto for Philosophy*, 20.
129 Jacques-Alain Miller, "La Suture (éléments de la logique du signifiant)," *Cahiers pour l'Analyse* 1 (1966): 39.
130 Miller, "La Suture," 41.
131 Miller, "La Suture," 39.
132 Miller, "La Suture," 41.
133 Miller, "La Suture," 44.
134 Ernest W. Retzlaff, "Embryological Development of the Cranium," in *The Cranium and Its Sutures: Anatomy, Physiology, Clinical Applications and Annotated Bibliography of Research in the Cranial Field*, ed. Ernest W. Retzlaff and Frederic L. Mitchell, Jr. (London: Springer, 1987), 3.
135 Slavoj Žižek, *Sex and the Failed Absolute* (London: Bloomsbury, 2020), 240.
136 Žižek, *Sex and the Failed Absolute*, 241.
137 Žižek, *Sex and the Failed Absolute*, 241.
138 Slavoj Žižek, "Suture: Forty Years Later," in *Concept and Form, Vol. 2: Interviews and Essays on "Cahiers pour L'Analyse,"* ed. Peter Hallward and Knox Peden (London: Verso, 2012), 157.
139 Deborah Sommer, "*Tian ren ganying*," in *Routledge Encyclopedia of Confucianism*, ed. Xinzhong Yao (London: Routledge, 2003), 614.
140 Dong Zongshu (attributed), *Luxuriant Gems of the Spring and Autumn*, ed. and trans. Sarah A. Queen and John S. Major (New York: Columbia University Press, 2016), 436. The number of days and joints is "rounded off to six whole sexagenary cycles."
141 Dong Zongshu (attributed), *Luxuriant Gems*, 435.

142 Aristotle, *Physics, Books 1–4*, trans. P. H. Wicksteed and F. M. Cornford, Loeb Classical Library (Cambridge, MA: Harvard University Press, 1929), 373. Henceforth cited in text as *Phys.*

143 Aristotle, *Physics*, 375.

144 Aristotle, *Physics*, 377.

145 Aristotle, *Physics*, 383.

146 Aristotle, *Physics*, 385.

147 *The Early Upanishads: Annotated Text and Translation*, trans. and ed. Patrick Olivelle (Oxford: Oxford University Press, 1998), 37. The *Brhadâranyaka Upanishad* is henceforth cited in text as *BU*.

148 *The Early Upanishads*, 39.

149 *The Early Upanishads*, 37. On the subject of Vedic sacrifices, Wendy Doniger (*On Hinduism* [Oxford: Oxford University Press, 2014]) writes: "Hindus, Buddhists and Jains all rejected the Vedic sacrifice, especially the animal sacrifice; but Hindus also dressed up their new doctrines and religious activities in the guise of the Vedic sacrifice. The previous sacrificial tradition was in this way made to appear as relatively inferior to newly revealed 'sacrifices.' But even anti-sacrificial traditions often found it necessary to call up the ancient category of sacrifice as a form of legitimation of the new in the guise of the old. New doctrines and practices were lent the air of archaic authority by being encoded in the vocabulary of sacrifice. Sacrifice, then, may function to conceptualize and articulate the new in terms of the old. The category serves to traditionalize innovations" (231).

150 *The Early Upanishads*, 37.

151 "Verily, this (brick-)built Fire-altar (Agni) is this (terrestrial) world:—the waters (of the encircling ocean) are its (circle of) enclosing-stones; the men its Yajushmatīs (bricks with special formulas); the cattle its Sūdadohas; the plants and trees its earth-fillings (between the layers of bricks), its oblations and fire-logs; Agni (the terrestrial fire) its Lokampṛṇā (space-filling brick);—thus this comes to make up the whole Agni, and the whole Agni comes to be the space-filler; and, verily, whosoever knows this, thus comes to be that whole (Agni) who is the space-filler." *The Satapatha-Brahmana*, according to the text of the Madhyandina school, translated by Julius Eggeling (Oxford: Clarendon Press, 1897), 381.

152 *Satapatha-Brahmana*, according to the text of the Madhyandina school, translated by Julius Eggeling (Oxford: Clarendon Press, 1897), 381

153 Charles Malamoud, *Cuire le monde: Rite et pensée dans l'Inde anceinne* (Paris: Éditions la Découverte, 1989), 67.

154 Patrick Olivelle, "Introduction," in *The Early Upanishads: Annotated Text and Translation*, trans. and ed. Patrick Olivelle (Oxford: Oxford University Press, 1998), 22.

155 Aristotle, *Physics*, 383.

156 G. W. F. Hegel, *The Science of Logic*, trans. and ed. George di Giovanni (Cambridge: Cambridge University Press, 2015), 59–60 [83].

157 Hegel, *Philosophy of Nature*, 35.

158 Hegel, *Philosophy of Nature*, 34 [10].

159 For an interpretation of Hegel's energy as actuality, see Marder, *Hegel's Energy: A Reading of "The Phenomenology of Spirit."*

160 Hegel, *Philosophy of Nature*, 36.

161 It is in absolute knowing that the joints of time and time as a joint converge: "Nonetheless, with regard to the *existence* of this concept [of spirit in its objectivity], *science* does not appear in time and in actuality until spirit has come round to itself as being this consciousness about itself [*Was aber das* Dasein *dieses Begriffs betrifft, so erscheint in der Zeit und Wirklichkeit die* Wissenschaft *nicht eher, als bis der Geist zu diesem Bewußtsein über sich gekommen ist*]" (Hegel, *PhG* §800).

162 Srebnik, *Concepts in Anatomy*, 123.

163 Martin Heidegger, "Letter on Humanism," in *Martin Heidegger: Basic Writings*, ed. David Farrell Krell (London: Routledge, 1993), 231–32.

164 "What is the pivot joint or atlantoaxial joint not insofar as it belongs to an organismic-vertebrate body, but to the subject or to the movement of thinking existence aspiring to turn away from the subject?" Such would be my question for Heidegger.

165 Slavoj Žižek, *Christian Atheism: How to Be a Real Materialist* (London: Bloomsbury, 2024), 75.

166 Henry James, *The Turn of the Screw*, ed. Peter G. Beidler (New York: St. Martin's Press, 1995), 108.

167 James, *The Turn of the Screw*, 116.

168 Shoshana Felman, "Turning the Screw of Interpretation," *Yale French Studies* 55/56: "Literature and Psychoanalysis. The Question of Reading: Otherwise" (1977): 64.

169 There is no time and no place for pivot joints in the products of understanding: that is the unacknowledged reason for the insufficiency of understanding within the dialectical framework and its overcoming at an early stage of Hegel's *Phenomenology*.

170 Augustine, *Confessions*, Loeb Classical Library, vol. 26 (Cambridge, MA: Harvard University Press, 1912), 65. Henceforth cited in text as *Conf.*

171 Augustine, *Confessions*, 89.

172 Augustine, *Confessions*, 87.

173 Augustine, *Confessions*, 159.

174 Augustine, *Confessions*, 161.

175 Augustine, *Confessions*, 161.

176 Augustine, *Confessions*, 173.

177 Augustine, *Confessions*, 177–79.

178 Augustine, *Confessions*, 198.

179 German *Kunst* points in a different direction, that of abilities, capabilities, or potentialities, *zu können*. The potentialities—of what? Of articulation?

180 I thank Boris Groys for this important reference.

181 Wassily Kandinsky, *Point and Line to Plane* (New York: Dover, 1979), 25.

182 Kandinsky, *Point and Line to Plane*, 31.

183 Boris Groys, "Introduction," in Alexander Kojève, *Kandinsky: Incarnating Beauty* (New York: David Zwirner Books, 2022), 15.

184 Kandinsky, *Point and Line to Plane*, 32.

185 Kandinsky, *Point and Line to Plane*, 32.

186 Kandinsky, *Point and Line to Plane*, 25.

187 Artemy Magun, *The Temptation of Non-Being: Negativity in Aesthetics* (New York: Bloomsbury, 2024), 44.

188 Magun, *The Temptation of Non-Being*, 44.

189 Magun, *The Temptation of Non-Being*, 160.

190 Martin Heidegger, "The Origin of the Work of Art," in *Martin Heidegger: Basic Writings*, ed. David Farrell Krell (London: Routledge, 1993), 167.

191 Jorge Oteiza, *Selected Writings*, ed. Joseba Zulaika (Reno: Center for Basque Studies, 2003), 202.

192 Oteiza, *Selected Writings*, 211.
193 Oteiza, *Selected Writings*, 311.
194 Ariel Kaplan, *Sefer Yetzirah: The Book of Creation* (San Francisco: Weiser Books, 1997), 22.
195 Burton Watson, *The Complete Works of Chuang Tzu* (New York: Columbia University Press, 1968), 131.
196 Laozi, *Daodejing*, trans. Edmund Ryden (Oxford: Oxford University Press, 2008), 25, translation modified.
197 To be sure, the practice of Oteiza's sculptural articulation, as the articulation of nothing, displays certain affinities with Chinese (particularly Taoist) thought. Besides the above-mentioned chapter from the *Daodejing*, the body, mapped across its joints and orifices in "Discussion on Making All Things Equal" in the writings of Zhuang Zhou (with which we have already engaged), is relevant to Oteiza's modernist articulation of nothing. While Zhuang Zhou's notions find expression in his method of perforation, the ideas from the *Daodejing* feed into the creation of empty spaces by the accumulation of units. His "final nothingness" is the first nothing, the *wù* of *Zhuangzi*, articulated by all that is. And this is not to mention the fact that Oteiza seems to have followed the prescription of chapter 9 in the *Daodejing* to the letter: "When tasks are done, then retire [退, *tuì*: retreat, withdraw, step back], that is the way of heaven" (Laozi, *Daodejing*, 21).
198 Laozi, *Daodejing*, 27.
199 Laozi, *The Classic of the Way and Virtue*, a new translation of the *Tao-te Ching* of Laozi as interpreted by Wang Bi, translated by Richard John Lynn (New York: Columbia University Press, 2004), 69.
200 Laozi, *Daodejing*, 101, translation modified.
201 Shuen-fu Lin, "A Good Place Need Not Be a Nowhere: The Garden and Utopian Thought in the Six Dynasties," in *Chinese Aesthetics: The Ordering of Literature, the Arts, and the Universe in the Six Dynasties*, ed. Zong-qi Cai (Honolulu: University of Hawai'i Press, 2004), 124.
202 Laozi, *Daodejing*, 77, translation modified.
203 Watson, *The Complete Works of Chuang Tzu*, 127, translation modified.
204 Watson, *The Complete Works of Chuang Tzu*, 142, translation modified.

205 Jamie Steinmetz et al., "Global, Regional, and National Burden of Osteoarthritis, 1990–2020 and Projections to 2050: A Systematic Analysis for the Global Burden of Disease Study 2021," *Lancet Rheumatology* 5, no. 9 (September 2023): E508–E522.

206 Loeser et al., "Osteoarthritis," 1697.

207 Theodor W. Adorno, *Negative Dialectics*, trans. E. B. Ashton (New York: Continuum, 1973), 158.

208 Yan Chen et al., "Abnormal Subchondral Bone Remodeling and Its Association with Articular Cartilage Degradation in Knees of Type 2 Diabetes Patients," *Bone Research* 5 (2017): 17034.

209 Carl Schmitt, *The Concept of the Political*, expanded edition, translated by George Schwab (Chicago: University of Chicago Press, 2007), 63.

210 Roberto Esposito, *Terms of the Political: Community, Immunity, Biopolitics*, trans. Rhiannon Noel Welch (New York: Fordham University Press, 2012).

211 Chantal Mouffe, "Carl Schmitt and the Paradox of Liberal Democracy," in *The Challenge of Carl Schmitt*, ed. Chantal Mouffe (London: Verso, 1999), 43–44, emphasis added.

212 "Damó xenus," in *Dictionary of Greek and Roman Biography and Mythology*, vol. 1, ed. William Smith (London: Taylor and Walton, 1844), 937.

213 Hermann Diels and Walther Kranz, *Die Fragmente der Vorsokratiker: Greichisch und Deutsch*, vol. 1 (Berlin: Wiedmannsche Verlagsbuchhandlung, 1960), 224.

214 Edmund Husserl, *Analyses Concerning Passive and Active Synthesis: Lectures on Transcendental Logic*, trans. Anthony Steinbock (Dordrecht: Kluwer Academic, 2001), 227.

215 Fernando Perez-Ruiz and Ana Maria Herrero-Beites, *Managing Gout in Primary Care* (New York: Springer, 2014), 2.

Index